Praise for *Declining Prospects*

"**W**hat a tour de force is *Declining Prospects!* This amazingly good, if salutary book, needs to be read not only by corporate lawyers, in-house counsel and lay clients, but also by law students and those who advise them. It has valuable lessons not only for the United States, but also for lawyers in other countries, particularly the United Kingdom. The book covers the extraordinary changes in the legal profession from the 1950s to the present day. The changes now taking place, which are described in such clear and interesting detail, could not have been predicted in 1976 or even as late as 1990. I could not disagree with any of Trotter's sobering conclusions on the future of the legal practice."

HIS HONOR JUDGE JOHN TOULMIN CMG QC FKC
Past President of the European Bar Council (CCBE), and Chairman of the Board of Trustees of the European Law Academy (ERA) 1997-2010, now Honorary Chairman for Life

"Mike Trotter may be the most well-informed and prescient current commentator on the economics and structure of organizations providing legal services to our nations' businesses. *Declining Prospects* pulls together a remarkable wealth of data on changes in large law firm economics and organization over recent decades and provides insightful analysis regarding the significance of these changes and the impact they may have on lawyers in and entering the profession. Whether his pessimism about the future of the highly-leveraged large commercial law firm is fully justified, only time will tell, but Trotter provides a factual basis for the intelligent reader to draw his or her own conclusions. For the young person considering law school and the possibility of a large-firm business law career, I cannot overstate the importance of reading and fully understanding *Declining Prospects.* As Trotter makes clear, the likelihood of a long-term high income career has declined while the costs of a legal education have escalated substantially. I believe every lawyer should give a copy of *Declining Prospects* to his favorite niece or young friend contemplating law school. I certainly will."

JOHN D. HOPKINS

Retired Executive Vice President and General Counsel of Jefferson Pilot Corporation, former leader of the Corporate and M&A Practices of King & Spalding, and Partner, Taylor English Duma LLP

"From the vantage point of a historian, economist and lawyer who personally has prospered from the phenomenal growth of the business of law, *Declining Prospects* author Mike Trotter tells us where the legal profession has been and where it's going. Not everyone will embrace the future he sees for lawyers, particularly the big law firms that have pushed partner profits to dizzying heights. While there's a bit of the scold in Trotter's analysis, he makes his best case for a changing business model for the profession when he falls back on his exhaustively detailed economic analysis of what happens when you have an increasing number of lawyers chasing a diminishing amount of work. For those contemplating their own future in the law, the message is clear: Enter the profession at your own risk and do it for the right reasons."

Ed Bean
Editor in Chief/Associate Publisher
The Daily Report   ALM

DECLINING PROSPECTS

*How Extraordinary Competition
and Compensation Are Changing
America's Major Law Firms*

Michael H. Trotter

ISBN: 1475053738

EAN-13: 9781475053739

Library of Congress Control Number: 2012905303

CreateSpace, North Charleston, SC

Michael H. Trotter received his law degree from the Harvard Law School in 1962, and his B.A, degree from Brown University *cum laude* (Phi Beta Kappa) in 1958. Prior to attending law school he was a Woodrow Wilson Fellow in the Harvard University Ph.D. Program in American History and was awarded a Master's Degree in History in 1959.

His study of law firm growth and change has combined the perspective of a historian, a successful practicing attorney and an experienced law firm manager. As a partner in two of the largest firms in America (the predecessors of Alston & Bird and of Kilpatrick, Townsend & Stockton) and three entrepreneurial law firms, he has been a keen student of the economics and ethos of modern law practice.

Mr. Trotter's 1997 book, *Profit and the Practice of Law – What's Happened to the Legal Profession*, has emerged as the definitive work on the major business practice law firms in America between 1960 and 1995. *Declining Prospects* and *Profit and the Practice of Law* together provide a consolidated history of growth and change in such law firms from the early fifties through 2010.

Mr. Trotter is a partner in the Atlanta, Georgia based law firm of Taylor English Duma LLP.

I dedicate this book to my present and former colleagues and mentors who taught me the practice of law and the principles of law firm management as well as the standards of ethics, professionalism and commitment to public service that have been, and I hope will continue to be, the hallmarks of our profession.

CONTENTS

PREFACE

y earlier book on the legal profession, *Profit and the Practice of Law: What's Happened to the Legal Profession,*[1] covered the period 1960 to 1995. It has emerged as the definitive work on growth and change in the legal profession in the United States in the latter portion of the 20th century. During the 35 years covered by the book, the law firms in the United States that represented the leading businesses transformed from small, prosperous, dignified, conservative, white-male professional partnerships into large, wealthy, aggressive, self-promoting, diverse business organizations with a dominant focus on making money.

Fifteen years have passed since the publication of *Profit and the Practice of Law,* but the important trends evident in the mid-1990s continue to exert their influence on the legal profession: the major

---

1 MICHAEL H. TROTTER, PROFIT AND THE PRACTICE OF LAW: WHAT'S HAPPENED TO THE LEGAL PROFESSION (1997).

business practice firms[2] are larger, more highly leveraged, more expensive, and more profitable to their equity partners. The practice of law has become an even more challenging and complicated undertaking. The major firms continue to increase their hourly billing rates and continue to emphasize billing more hours at these higher hourly rates. Alternative fee arrangements remain more talk than reality. In-house corporate law departments have become ubiquitous, much larger, and thoroughly competent.

Like *Profit and the Practice of Law*, this book concerns itself primarily with the major business practice firms providing legal services to major business clients, but the growing importance of corporate law departments requires significant attention as well. The major firm lawyers and their firms are no longer at the apex of the profession. Corporate general counsel—the senior lawyers who are full-time employees of their companies—now serve as the conductors of their own legal orchestras and have gained significant influence over the profession. Many of them are very well-paid.[3]

The economic impact of the legal profession on the economy of the United States is much greater than most people, including most lawyers, realize. As of 2010, there was about one lawyer for every 252 people in the United States.[4] About one of every 116 people employed

2 Most of the largest and most prestigious law firms in America are usually referred to as "corporate firms" because the primary clients are businesses that historically have been organized as corporations. I prefer to call them "major business practice firms" because of the variety of business organization models used by their clients in the 21st century. Today, the law firms themselves are often organized as limited liability partnerships (LLPs).

3 Katheryn Hayes Tucker, *The South's Richest General Counsel*, FULTON CNTY. DAILY REP., Nov. 21, 2011, *available at* http://www.law.com/jsp/cc/PubArticleCC. jsp?id=1202532907861 (reporting that the highest paid corporate General Counsel of a Southeastern U.S. company earned $9,200,000 in fiscal year 2010 and 140 earned at least $1,000,000 a year).

4 Am. Bar. Ass'n, Lawyer Demographics (2011), http://www.americanbar. org/content/dam/aba/migrated/marketresearch/PublicDocuments/lawyer_ demographics_2011.authcheckdam.pdf (showing that there were 1,225,452 lawyers in the United States at the end of 2010); *U.S. Census Bureau Announces*

in the United States is a lawyer[5] (and for every lawyer law firms usually employ one or more persons to support their practices). In 2003 law offices generated $180 billion in revenues. These revenues represented about 18% of the professional services sector and four percent of the services sector. They greatly exceed those of management consulting firms ($89 billion), CPA firms ($53 billion), and advertising agencies ($26 billion). Between 1998 and 2003 law office revenues grew more than those of CPA firms and broker/dealer firms.[6]

I began the practice of law in 1960 in Atlanta as a "summer boarder" at Alston, Sibley, Miller, Spann & Shackelford following my first year in law school. The firm became Alston, Miller & Gaines (the predecessor firm of Alston & Bird) before I started as an associate in the summer of 1962. In 1967 I became a partner and at various times I served as the head of the firm's recruiting committee, its facilities committee and as chair of its corporate practice group. In 1977, because of a severe client conflict, I joined with friends to form a new firm named Trotter, Bondurant, Griffin, Miller & Hishon. Subsequently I started another firm in 1982, Trotter, Smith & Jacobs, which survived until 1992. I then joined Kilpatrick & Cody (now Kilpatrick Townsend & Stockton LLP) in September of 1992, and retired from the firm at the end of 2005.

In January 2009 I was attracted out of retirement to become a partner in Taylor English Duma LLP, a "New Model" law firm of

2010 Census Population Counts, U.S. CENSUS BUREAU (Dec. 21, 2010), http://2010.census.gov/news/releases/operations/cb10-cn93.html (showing that U.S. population was 308,745,538 in 2010).

5 Household Data Annual Averages, BUREAU OF LABOR STATISTICS (2010), http://www.bls.gov/cps/cpsaat11.pdf (showing a total of 139,064,000 employed people in the United States in 2010).

6 Analysis of Legal Profession and Law Firms, HARVARD LAW SCHOOL: PROGRAM ON THE LEGAL PROFESSION (last accessed Dec. 23, 2011), http://www.law.harvard.edu/programs/plp/pages/statistics.php (providing various statistical data on legal profession).

approximately 45 lawyers. The firm emphasizes high quality services, low leverage, and low overhead. The cost savings inherent in its model are passed on to clients resulting in lower costs for the services the firm provides. Consequently clients have found this new model to be very attractive. During a time when many law firms were laying off lawyers, Taylor English has grown from four lawyers in 2006 to more than 100 lawyers in December of 2011. Most of its lawyers have significant experience in the practice of law. Taylor English was recently ranked the fastest growing law firm in Atlanta and the 10th largest in Atlanta in terms of number of attorneys.[7]

My experience has included serving as a partner in two firms that were among the 100 largest in the United States (referred to as the Am Law 100)[8] and in three entrepreneurial law firms. Exposure to this diverse group of firms has allowed me to learn first-hand how major business practice firms have grown and changed in the United States over the last 50 years. I've had the opportunity to work with many fine lawyers in a number of the United States' largest and best known firms. These firms include Breed Abbott, Blank Rome, Cadwalader, Cahill Gordon, Chadbourne & Parke, Cleary Gottlieb, Clifford Turner (now Clifford Chance), Cravath, Davis Polk, Kaye Scholer, King & Spalding, Paul Weiss, Piper & Marbury (now DLA Piper), Shearman & Sterling, Simpson Thatcher, Skadden, Sullivan & Cromwell, Trubin Sillcocks, and Weil Gotshal among others.

---

7 *Atlanta's Top Law Firms,* ATLANTA BUS. CHRON., April 27, 2012.

8 *The American Lawyer's* "Am Law 100" identifies the 100 firms headquartered in the United States with the largest gross revenues from legal work listed in the order of their gross revenues. The Am Law 200 lists the next 100 firms based on their gross revenues. The term "Am Law 100" is used herein to denote the top 100 firms and "Am Law 200" is used to denote all 200 firms that appear on one or the other of the lists. Both the Alston firm and the Kilpatrick firm have consistently been ranked in the Am Law 100.

I have also had the opportunity to hone and test my observations about law firm management and economics issues through writing, dialoguing and teaching. I was fortunate to be able to participate in the American Bar Association's *Second Seize the Future* Conference in 1999 and in its *Raise the Bar* Colloquium in 2005. In addition to *Profit and the Practice of Law*, I wrote *Pig in a Poke? The Uncertain Advantages of Very Large and Highly Leveraged Law Firms in America*, which appeared as a chapter in the American Bar Association's publication, *Raise the Bar – Real World Solutions for a Troubled Profession (2007)*.[9] I have been a columnist for *The Daily Report* in Atlanta since 1990 writing numerous columns on law firm management and economics.[10] I taught two courses in the mid-1990s at the Emory University Law School on law firm management and economics that apparently were among the first such courses taught at a major U.S. law school.[11]

Much of the factual information from the 1960s and 1970s that provided the basis for *Profit and the Practice of Law* was not available in the public domain. While the task of commenting on and analyzing the profession in more recent times has been greatly facilitated by *The American Lawyer, The National Law Journal* and Atlanta's own *Daily Report*, it is still not easy to gain access to accurate inside information.

---

9 Michael H. Trotter, *Pig in a Poke? The Uncertain Advantages of Very Large and Highly Leveraged Law Firms in America, in* RAISE THE BAR: REAL WORLD SOLUTIONS FOR A TROUBLED PROFESSION 33 (Lawrence J. Fox, ed., 2007).

10 *See also* Michael H. Trotter, Address at the Corporate Counsel Law Section and Corporate Counsel Committee of Younger Lawyers Section of State Bar of Georgia Luncheon (Feb. 27, 1990), *as reprinted in* FULTON CNTY. DAILY REP., Mar. 5 1990.

11 Comment by William D. Henderson, *Name the Missing Law School Course*, ADAM SMITH, ESQ: AN INQUIRY INTO THE ECONOMICS OF LAW FIRMS, (last accessed June 12, 2010), http://www.adamsmithesq.com/archives/2005/09/name-the-missin. html.

I am indebted to my former colleagues Bill Jacobs, Phil Moise, and Paul Bellows, and my present colleagues David Baker, Al Hill, John Hopkins and Marc Taylor for having read drafts of this book and for their useful comments that greatly improved it. I am equally indebted to my daughter An Trotter, the Director of Administration for the Law Department of Viacom, for her many insights and suggestions that have markedly improved the presentation with respect to corporate law departments. The book has benefited significantly from the able work of Rob Gignilliat, an honor student at the University of Georgia Law School and an editor of the school's law review, who worked with me as a research and editorial assistant. Nevertheless, I am solely responsible of the opinions expressed herein.

Michael H. Trotter
mtrotter@taylorenglish.com
http://trotterlawandeconomics.com
Atlanta, Georgia
June 8, 2012

INTRODUCTION

For longer than I care to admit, I have predicted that the inflation-adjusted profitability of most of the major business practice law firms in the United States would decline. While average Profits Per Partner ("PPP")[1] adjusted for inflation did decline for many of the major firms during the early 1990s, they again surged upwards beginning in 1996.[2] Another decline began in 2008 as a result in part of the Great Recession.[3] For the various reasons set forth in this book, I believe that the decline is likely to continue and

---

1 Profits per partner is calculated by dividing net operating income by the number of equity partners. *A Guide to Our Methodology,* AM. LAW., May 2010, at 123.

2 *See infra* Chapter 2.

3 Profits Per Partner of the Am Law 100 firms dropped 4.3 percent in 2008, and revenue per lawyer dropped 1.2 percent, *Lessons of the Am Law 100,* AM. LAW, May 2009, at 107.

will only increase in severity in the years ahead for many of the major business practice firms.

The legal profession in the United States is very large and diverse; there are many sizes and types of firms each with its own strengths and weaknesses. Demographic information compiled by the ABA shows that 76% of all lawyers in private practice are employed in law firms with fewer than twenty lawyers, and 48% are in solo practice.[4] And like every other industry, the legal profession is affected by continuing changes in business practices, financial realities, and technology.

It will be as difficult for major law firm lawyers to see the writing on the wall as it has been for travel agents, stock brokers, insurance agents, newspaper editors and the many others whose occupations have experienced transformational changes in recent years. While I expect that there will be a significant reduction in the profitability of many major business practice law firms, I have no doubt that the legal profession will continue to prosper, but not nearly as much as it has during the last 20 years.

Young people need to know where the profession is headed, not just where it has been. Those entering the legal profession will find that there are real choices to be made among law firms and practice models. Good and diverse opportunities will remain for large numbers of lawyers to enjoy stimulating, satisfying and profitable careers in the United States. Most will not make *The American Lawyer's* "Litigator of the Month" or "Deal of the Month" Clubs or work for an Am Law 200 firm, but many will be satisfied just the same.

The law firms in the United States receiving most of the publicity and media attention are the so called "Am Law 200" which are the 200 firms with the greatest gross revenues identified annually by *The*

---

4 Am. Bar. Ass'n, Lawyer Demographics (2009), http://www.americanbar.org/content/dam/aba/migrated/marketresearch/PublicDocuments/Lawyer_Demographics.authcheckdam.pdf (referencing year 2000 data).

American Lawyer magazine.[5] These firms had 110,441 lawyers in 2009 and accounted for about nine percent of the lawyers admitted to practice in the United States.[6] Most of the lawyers working at these firms are very well compensated.

There are many largely unnoticed medium-sized and smaller firms whose lawyers are also very well compensated. Often their working conditions are more amiable than those in major firms and their practice model is more appealing to younger lawyers with "quality of life" concerns. The growing diversity of practice models in the legal services industry benefits both clients and private practice lawyers. No single size or model fits all.

In the accounting industry there are only four big firms and several secondary ones, but there are thousands of other small accounting firms providing services to small businesses, families and individuals, and there are thousands more accountants working in-house for their employers. There is likely to be increased concentration and stratification among the major business practice law firms, but we will still be a long way from having only four dominant firms. Because of conflicts of interest and the many legal jurisdictions within the United States, we are very unlikely to see such extreme concentration at the top end of the legal profession in the foreseeable future. We will continue to have firms of all sizes and many, many small firms and sole practitioners just as we do today. Some smaller law firms will

---

5 *See supra* note 8 (providing definition of Am Law 100 and 200).

6 *Gross Revenue Takes A Fall: 2009 Gross Revenue*, AM. LAW., June 2010, at 95-100 (providing Am Law 200 rankings for the fiscal year 2009 and listing the number of lawyers for each firm); *Baker & McKenzie Tops Skadden: 2009 Gross Revenue*, AM. LAW., May 2010, at 137-38 (providing Am Law 100 rankings for the fiscal year 2009 and listing number of lawyers for each firm); AM. BAR. ASS'N, LAWYER DEMOGRAPHICS (2009), http://www.americanbar.org/content/dam/aba/migrated/marketresearch/PublicDocuments/Lawyer_Demographics.authcheckdam.pdf (stating that total number of lawyers in 2009 was 1,180,386).

be able to build on the loyalty of their clients to grow as their clients grow and to become larger firms representing major businesses. This is the way that many firms of 20 lawyers or less grew during the 1960s and 1970s and became Am Law 200 firms of today.

Because of aggressive national competition for the representation of major businesses, it will not be as easy to grow today as it was then. Further, the increasingly oligopolistic banking, investment banking, private equity and accounting businesses often encourage their clients to use their friends in the legal world. The concentration of major business advisory services in the hands of a small number of banks, investment banks, investment funds and accounting firms has contributed significantly to the increasing size of many U.S. law firms.

The major business practice portion of the legal profession continues to wrestle with its own challenges. It is fundamentally divided between lawyers who buy legal services and lawyers who sell them. The lawyers who buy are predominantly corporate counsel and their law departments and those who sell are private practice lawyers and their firms. Growth in the number and competence of lawyers practicing in the United States, and growth in the size and strength of corporate law departments continue to be the most important developments in the profession.

The existence of capable and knowledgeable lawyers on the buyer's side has fundamentally changed the lawyer-client relationship between the major business practice firms and their clients. Corporate counsel have been slow to realize and utilize the enormous power and control they have over private practice firms. For many, their attitudes have been influenced by their own origins as practicing lawyers in private practice, and most continue to have important relationships within the ranks of private practice lawyers and the law firms from which they came. These relationships can serve or conflict with the interests of the companies for which they work.

Corporate counsel read about the extraordinary profitability of their private practice counterparts in the legal press; they are also aware of the rising costs of legal services associated with such profitability. They are under growing pressure from their corporate employers to reduce these costs just as their companies seek to reduce other costs. As a result, corporate counsel are expected and empowered by their employers to rein in the costs of using the major business practice firms and their lawyers.

Professor Clayton Christensen of the Harvard Business School has noticed that: "Large American law firms are just about the most profitable businesses in the world."[7] Corporate counsel and their employers have also taken note. Some lawyers no doubt scoff at Professor Christensen's comment. Very few lawyers, even at the best firms, earn as much as the CEOs of large national and international businesses. On the other hand, very few such businesses have dozens, if not hundreds, of senior officers with average incomes in excess of a million dollars a year.

In 2010 there were 67 U.S. law firms whose annual average Profits Per Partner exceeded $1 million (an aggregate of 12,508 equity partners).[8] In addition, many partners in smaller firms also enjoy compensation in excess of $1 million a year. In recent decades there have been very few other careers that could offer smart and

---

7 [18] Mark Chandler, Gen. Counsel of Cisco, Address at Northwestern School of Law Securities Regulation Institute: State of Technology in Law (2007) (quoting Clayton M. Christensen), *available at* http://techlawmarketing.blogspot.com/2007/05/cisco-gc-on-how-law-firms-must-change.html; *see also Cisco General Counsel on the State of Technology in the Law*, INHOUSE BLOG (Mar. 21, 2007) (noting that the speech is a "must-read for in-house lawyers").

8 *The Am Law 100: 2010*, AM. LAW., May 2011, at 139-149.

ambitious students such promising odds of a highly prosperous and stable career. These highly successful and highly compensated lawyers are nonetheless a fortunate few. If half of the equity partners in these 67 firms (6,254 partners) earned a million dollars a year they would represent about one-half of one percent of the 1,225,000 lawyers admitted to practice in the United States in 2010.[9]

This book will focus on the major business practice firms and on the corporate counsel who are now responsible for employing most of them. These firms are the richest and most examined part of the legal profession. As legal advisors to the largest businesses in the world they have a great influence inside and outside the profession and they share the leadership of the legal profession with corporate counsel, but increasingly corporate counsel have become the senior partners.

Most of the information presented and analyzed in this book focuses on major business practice firms including those in New York City, the principal center of the business practice in the United States, and in Atlanta, Georgia where I have practiced law for 50 years and which is the market I know best.

Before examining how the legal profession in the United States has been transformed since 1950, a brief review of the simplicity of law firm economics is in order. The basic economic principles of major business practice law firms are as follows:

1. The major firms are owned and managed by their equity partners.

2. The equity partners provide legal services to clients themselves and hire other lawyer-employees (nonequity partners, counsel, associates, staff attorneys, contract attorneys, etc.) and other billable non-lawyer professionals (paralegals, docket clerks, investigators,

9 Am. Bar. Ass'n, Lawyer Demographics (2011), http://www.americanbar. org/content/dam/aba/migrated/marketresearch/PublicDocuments/lawyer_ demographics_2011.authcheckdam.pdf (showing that there were 1,225,453 lawyers in the United States at the end of 2010).

etc.) to work for their firms and to provide legal services to clients in return for the payment of fees by the clients.

3. Firms collect fees from clients to pay the firm's employees and operating expenses, and split the remainder among the equity partners.

4. Hourly rates remain the predominant basis for determining fees, but in recent years an increased amount of attention has been paid to alternative means of determining the amount of compensation to be paid.

5. The firms typically spend 50% to 70% of their gross revenues for employees and other operating expenses.

6. Of course, the law firms have to collect from their clients for the work they perform, and to the extent they do not, the uncollected revenue reduces equity partner compensation.

7. Firms are able to increase their Profits Per Partner in several ways. They can:

- charge their clients more for the work they do either by increasing their hourly billing rates (if they bill by the hour) or by increasing their payments from clients through alternative fee arrangements;
- do more work for their clients by working more hours or by using more lawyers (and other billable personnel);
- acquire new clients, which will increase the number of hours they can bill; and
- reduce their overhead by paying less rent, restraining the compensation of their lawyer-employees and other personnel, having a smaller support staff, and managing their business in a more efficient way.

8. Most major firms hire people who are not lawyers to do some of the work of managing and administering the enterprise that otherwise would have to be done by lawyers with the expectation that

the amount paid to these additional employees will be less than what the lawyers can earn for the additional time they can bill to clients.

9. Most Am Law 100 firms realize profit margins of 30% to 40% of their gross revenues as compensation to the equity partners.[10] A few elite firms enjoy substantially higher profit margins, and a few others have profit margins below 30%.

Most major business practice firms in the United States have adopted what is often referred to as the New York Model: a large and highly leveraged firm with relatively few equity partners and a relatively large number of lawyer-employees, high charges by the hour or otherwise, and high billable hour requirements – all supported by a large staff of non-lawyer support personnel. Most of the major firms outside of New York City have attempted to emulate this model.

High leverage means there are many more lawyer-employees than equity partners. The leverage ratio increases when a firm increases the number of its lawyer-employees relative to the number of its equity partners. For example, leverage of 1 to 1 indicates there is one such lawyer-employee for every equity partner in the firm. Leverage of 2 to 1 indicates that there are two such employees for each partner. Conversely, a leverage ratio of 0.5 to 1 indicates two equity partners for each lawyer-employee. Firms have also increased their leverage by adding non-lawyer employees whose services can be billed to clients, including paralegals, librarians, investigators, docket clerks and others. The "Leverage Ratios" used herein refer only to the ratios of lawyer-employees to equity partners.

---

10 In 1990, the average profit margin of the Am Law 100 was 36.54%. This has remained relatively unchanged over time. In 2000, the average profit margin was 36.08% and, in 2009, it was 35.84%. *See The Efficiency Equation: 2009 Profitability Index*, AM. LAW., May 2010, at 169-70 (providing profit margin data for Am Law 100 in fiscal year 2009); *Measuring Up: Profitability Index*, AM. LAW., July 2001, at 192-93 (providing profit margin data in fiscal year 2000); *The Am Law 100: Ranked by Am Law Profitability Index*, AM. LAW., July/Aug. 1991, at 46-51 (providing profit margin data fiscal year 1990).

Equity partner compensation can be increased by charging higher rates or fees, working more billable hours, increasing leverage by adding additional billable personnel without a corresponding increase in the number of equity partners, or by controlling overhead. While it is as simple as that, there are market forces and human limitations that constrain what can be done with each of these "levers."

For decades most of the major firms have 1) steadily increased their charges (hourly rates or otherwise) in excess of inflation, 2) hired larger numbers of lawyer-employees and non-lawyer personnel to charge to clients (increased leverage), 3) required all of their billable personnel to work more hours chargeable to clients, 4) charged some overhead expenses directly to clients, and 5) periodically made efforts to moderate the growth of overhead expenses.

While the New York Model has significantly increased the average PPP of the equity partners in the major firms, it has also produced many undesirable "side effects." We will seek in the following chapters to identify and quantify the changes that have led to extraordinary financial returns for the equity partners of the New York Model firms as well as the side effects. We will also explore the burgeoning "New Model" law firm movement.

PART I

THE TRANSFORMATION OF THE MAJOR BUSINESS PRACTICE LAW FIRMS IN THE UNITED STATES

CHAPTER ONE

The Transformation – 1950 to 1990

The transformation of the major business practice firms in the United States began slowly around 1960 and has continued to this day. Before explaining the current conditions and prospects for the legal profession in the United States in later chapters, it is important to explore how and why the profession has changed so much since the 1950s.

MAJOR BUSINESS PRACTICE FIRMS IN 1950 AND HOW THEY GREW

To begin with, most law firms in the 1940s and 1950s were not financially attractive places to earn a living. Between 1940 and 1960 lawyers' incomes, adjusted for inflation, actually declined. In 1958 a Special Committee on the Economics of Law Practice created by the American Bar Association issued a report entitled *The 1958 Lawyer and His 1938 Dollar*. The report stated:

3

The percentage of the national income spent for legal services has dwindled to about one-third of what it was 25 years ago, in spite of the increased complexities of business and taxation. Do you know that the national average income of self-employed persons (excluding farmers) rose 144% during that period? Incomes of dentists rose 83%. Our colleagues in the medical profession have enjoyed a steep climb in net earnings of 157%. Yet during that same period the income of lawyers in private practice has risen a mere 58%.[1]

The 58% increase fell far short of the inflation of 123% that occurred between 1933 and 1958. The situation was so bad that between 1949 and 1959 the number of students in law school declined by 25% while the country's population was increasing by 20%.[2] In 1964 an article published in *Law Office Economics and Management* concluded that: "Statistics and the results of many surveys in the fifties revealed that the legal profession . . . was rapidly becoming an impoverished profession."[3]

It was estimated that there were 212,605 lawyers in the United States in 1950: one for every 709 persons in the country.[4] There

---

1 George B. Shepherd, The Economics of Pretrial Discovery: Theory, Empirical Analysis, and Historical Impact (Sept. 2009), at 130 (unpublished Ph.D dissertation, Stanford University), available at http://gradworks.umi.com/3382952. pdf (quoting *Inventory of the Legal Profession: Lawyers Can Take Lessons from Doctors*, 38 A.B.A. J. 196,196-99 (1952)).

2 *Id.* at 130-131.

3 *Id.* at 132 (quoting Henry L. Jordan, *A Time Billing System*, 5 L. OFF. ECON. & MGMT. 37, 37 (1964)).

4 Robert M. Segal & John Fei, *The Economics of the Legal Profession: An Analysis by States*, 39 A.B.A. J. 110, 113 (1953).

were approximately 1,225,000 licensed lawyers in the country in 2010:[5] approximately one for each 252 persons.[6] In 1950 most of the major business practice firms in the United States were very small in comparison to today's firms. Most had fewer associates than partners (very low leverage) and modest overhead. Most did not bill for their services by the hour. They were small for a good reason. Most were organized as general partnerships and the personal assets of every partner were on the line to pay any obligations of the partnership. As a result lawyers did not want to be in a partnership with people they did not know well and trust implicitly. These risks were significantly reduced by the purchase of lawyers' professional liability insurance which became common place in the 1960s. They were further reduced in the 1990s by the conversion of most law firm partnerships into limited liability partnerships.

The following charts compare the 1950 size and leverage of some well-known U.S. law firms in selected U.S. cities to the size and leverage of these same firms (some augmented by mergers) in 2009.[7]

The first chart shows the total number of lawyers in each firm. As is evident from the chart, in 1950 most of the firms listed were very small by today's standards and in 2009 most were more than 20 times larger.

---

5 AM. BAR. ASS'N, LAWYER DEMOGRAPHICS (2011), http://www.americanbar.org/content/dam/aba/migrated/marketresearch/PublicDocuments/lawyer_demographics_2011.authcheckdam.pdf.

6 *U.S. Census Bureau Announces 2010 Census Population Counts*, U.S. CENSUS BUREAU (Dec. 21, 2010), http://2010.census.gov/news/releases/operations/cb10-cn93.html (showing that U.S. population was 308,745,538 in 2010).

7 For information about firm size and leverage in 1950, I have relied upon the 1950 Martindale-Hubbell Law Directory. For recent size and leverage, I have relied upon the Am Law 100 and Am Law 200 Reports. *See Gross Revenue Takes A Fall: 2009 Gross Revenue*, AM. LAW., June 2010, at 95-96 (providing Am Law 200 size and leverage data for fiscal year 2009); *Baker & McKenzie Tops Skadden: 2009 Gross Revenue*, AM. LAW., May 2010, at 137-38 (providing Am Law 100 size and leverage data for fiscal year 2009).

Size (Number of Lawyers) Comparison: 1950 to 2009

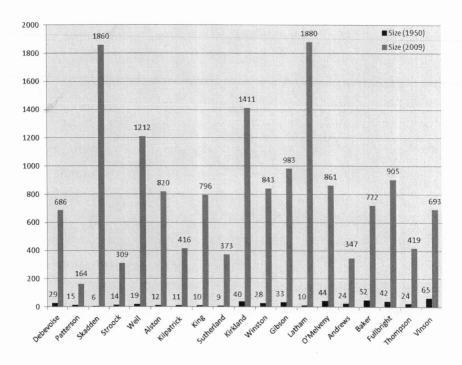

New York	Atlanta	Chicago	L.A.	Texas

The second chart reflects the increase in the use of lawyer-employee leverage by the same law firms between 1950 and 2009. Virtually all of the lawyer-employees in 1950 were "associates." In recent decades law firms have also increased leverage by the addition of other categories of lawyer-employees including nonequity partners, senior counsel, counsel, senior associates, associates, staff attorneys, and contract lawyers as well as billable non-lawyer personnel (such as legal assistants). Note, however, that their additional non-lawyer leverage is not reflected in the chart below.

Leverage Comparison: 1950 to 2009

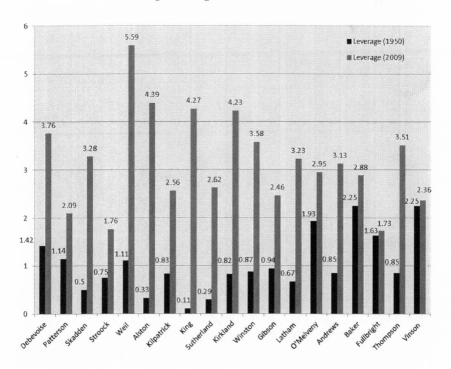

New York	Atlanta	Chicago	L.A.	Texas

Leverage ratios increased for most of the firms between 1950 and 2009 in the range of 100 to 500% or more, although several firms in Texas with unusually high leverage ratios in 1950 have seen only modest increases in leverage while growing considerably in size.

CHANGES IN THE MAJOR FIRMS BETWEEN 1960 AND 1990

The major business practice firms were much the same in 1960 as they had been in 1950. Shearman, Sterling & Wright with 125 lawyers was the largest law firm in the United States in 1960. There were two other firms in New York City with more than 100 lawyers and 17 firms outside New York City with more than 50 lawyers. The largest law firm in Atlanta, Georgia in 1960 had 21 lawyers and the next largest had 16.[8] The view of what constitutes a "large" law firm or a "highly leveraged" firm has changed significantly as a result of the tremendous growth in size of major business practice firms and in the leverage utilized by them.

Most firms had two categories of lawyers: partners and associates. And most firms had an "up or out" policy: associates who did not become partners within five or six years in Atlanta or 7 or 8 years in New York City were assisted in finding other employment or asked to leave. A few New York firms had a few "permanent associates."

In the early 1960s the major law firms were stable and prosperous organizations, but much smaller and much less leveraged than the major firms today. There were very few in-house lawyers and even fewer corporate law departments in those days: the outside firms functioned as the law departments of most of their clients. The partners usually had direct access to top management and often were good friends of their clients' executives.

The partners in such firms were well paid by then-existing standards, but few became rich from their legal practices alone.[9]

---

8 *Martindale-Hubbell Law Directory*, 1960.

9 The Schedule of Minimum Fees of the Atlanta Bar Association, May 1, 1962 (a month before I started practicing law in Atlanta) stated in part that: "There was also demonstrated that income of the legal profession had dropped below that of other professions in the community and that the income of the average Atlanta lawyer had dropped below the income of lawyers in other comparable cities. It is the purpose of this schedule to make a timely revision of the previous Minimum Fee Schedule and also to correct the disparity of income of the legal profession in Atlanta and to help bring the income of Atlanta lawyers in line with the income received by lawyers in other comparable cities. In doing this a basis has been adopted that will accord a more realistic valuation of the time required in rendering legal services."

Inherited wealth, prosperous spouses, shrewd investments in the stock market (and in clients), service as corporate officers and directors, and successful real estate speculation were among the factors that could and did affect the wealth and lifestyles of these lawyers. The rising prosperity of the United States following World War II lifted many a lawyer's boat.

During the 1960s most law firms did not make a conscious decision to grow in size. Growth came about primarily because the growing post-war economy resulted in many new businesses and many growing old ones. In addition, the increasing reliance on law and regulation to manage the economies of the United States and the world increased the need for legal advice and support. As a result, there was a significant increase in the amount of legal work to be done, but not enough lawyers in practice or students in law school to serve the growing needs of business clients.

The scarcity of lawyers was a result of stagnation in the size of the legal profession for almost 30 years following the start of the Great Depression. A stagnant economy, poor law practice economics, a drop in the birth rate during these years, and the large number of young people who went to war (many of whom did not return) all had an impact. In 1960 many major law firms had more partners between the ages of 50 and 65 than between the ages of 35 and 50. There were more senior partners headed for retirement than there were junior partners available to take their place, even if the firms did not grow their practices.

The shortage of new lawyers, combined with the growing needs of business, created exceptional opportunities for law school graduates in the 1960s. Good students from top law schools had multiple job offers from major firms, rapidly increasing compensation, and high-percentage prospects of a partnership within five to eight years.

In the 1960s, the lateral movement of partners or associates from one firm to another was frowned upon and rarely occurred. Consequently, the only way a firm could provide the additional services needed by its growing clientele was to work its lawyers harder and to hire at the entry level more new associates to be developed as quickly as possible. During the 1960s and early 1970s, if a major business practice firm wanted to meet the rising demand for legal services, it had to do so by adding new associates fresh from law school.

The revenues produced in the 1960s by the higher level of activity and the swelling ranks of associates resulted in higher compensation for partners. Growth and the resulting leverage drove profitability, rather than the desire for profitability driving growth and leverage.

The firms found that growth was both necessary and profitable. With sufficient new business to support more lawyers and higher associate-partner ratios, many firms continued to grow and prosper by enlarging their workforce of young associates. In the process, associate leverage in most major firms was slowly but steadily increasing along with partner compensation.

Greatly increased profitability was inevitable when the firms started growing rapidly to meet the growing need for legal services. It was a natural result of a growing cadre of young lawyers working at relatively low salaries generating billable hours chargeable to clients at substantial profit margins. In the process, firms that had been in operation for years with a ratio of several partners to each associate found themselves with one, or two, or in some cases three or more associates working and generating profits for each partner.

Because so many new associates were hired during the 1960s and early 1970s, and because such a high percentage of them became partners, most of the major firms were faced with hiring even more associates in the later 1970s in order to maintain or increase their existing leverage and the related partner compensation levels. At some point in the 1970s or 1980s (depending on the characteristics of the individual firms and the cities in which they were located), the naturally occurring growth in size, leverage and profitability took on a life of its own. Growth began to occur for growth's sake; the desire for greater equity partner profits began to drive the need for increased size and leverage.

Among the other factors contributing to the transformation of the legal profession in the United States in the thirty-five years between 1960 and 1995 were:

- growth in the number and capability of lawyers licensed to practice in U.S.,
- growth in number, size and competence of corporate law departments,
- as already noted in the preceding charts, growth in size and leverage of the major business practice firms,
- advent of several additional categories of lawyer-employees (nonequity partner, counsel, senior counsel, senior associate), so that firms that had operated for decades with only two categories of lawyers evolved into much more complex organizations with multiple categories of lawyer-employees,
- increased use of hourly billing rates to determine legal fees,
- tracking of lawyer timesheets and establishing billable hour requirements for all lawyers,
- extraordinary increases in associate compensation,
- relaxation of marketing restrictions on law firms,
- more specialization and narrower categories of specialization,
- opening of the profession to women and minorities,
- developing technology,
- actions taken by law firms to increase the number of billable hours that they could charge to their clients,

- increasing respectability of lateral movement by partners and associates among law firms and in-house law departments,
- introduction of multiple categories of billable non-lawyer personnel including paralegals, legal assistants, various categories of clerks (docket, file management, etc.) and other assistants, and
- availability of reliable information concerning the profitability of the various major firms.

These 1960-1995 trends are explored in greater depth in my previous book on the transformation of the legal profession, *Profit and the Practice of Law.*[10]

The number of lawyers admitted to practice in the United States grew from approximately 212,600 in 1950 to approximately 1,225,000 in 2010. This significant growth in the supply of lawyers in the United States will be discussed in greater length in Chapter Seven: Competition – An Abundant Supply of Capable Lawyers and Law Firms. During the same period there was a significant increase in the number and size of corporate law departments as discussed in Chapter Ten: The Rise of Corporate Counsel.

HOURLY RATES

The growing use of hourly rates to determine legal charges to clients was a factor that significantly affected the legal profession. During the fifties and sixties many major firms did not record the time invested in client work by their lawyers. Of those that did, many

---

10 *See* MICHAEL H. TROTTER, PROFIT AND THE PRACTICE OF LAW: WHAT'S HAPPENED TO THE LEGAL PROFESSION 1-60 (1997).

used it as one point of reference out of several in determining an appropriate fee in a particular matter.

By the early 1970s most major business practice firms had adopted hourly billing for most of their work and kept track of the time invested in a client's project as the principal determinator of the value of the service rendered. One of my senior partners at the Alston firm had worked at Davis Polk prior to World War II and told me that its lawyers had kept time even then. He was responsible for bringing the practice to the Alston firm after the War. Although the firm's lawyers recorded their time on both client and firm matters when I worked as a "summer border" in 1960, the time was used as only one factor to be considered in determining a client bill, and was not used at all in the management of the firm and its lawyers.

Most firms that had not already started charging for their services by the hour began to do so during the 1960s and early 1970s. Ironically, clients often initiated the change to billing by the hour. It was Chrysler that first insisted on hourly billing at the Alston firm in the mid-1960s. Hourly rates were usually based on years in practice and were regularly increased in increments on an annual basis. Little did clients or their outside lawyers know how much this decision would affect the future of law firm economics.

Some bar associations had "minimum fee schedules." Habitually charging less than the standard fee could subject the violator to discipline for unethical conduct.[11] As discussed in greater detail in *Profit and the Practice of Law*, as hourly rates increased and the

---

11 Schedule of Minimum Fees of the Atlanta Bar Association, Adopted by the Atlanta Bar Association Effective May 1, 1962. The schedule quoted with favor Opinion 302 of the Committee on Professional Ethics of the American Bar Association adopted November 27, 1961 to the effect that: "The habitual charging of fees less than those established by a minimum fee schedule, or the charging of such fees without proper justification, may be evidence of unethical conduct." Most lawyers today have never seen or heard of a minimum fee schedule.

amount of time utilized to complete projects also increased, the cost of legal services to clients increased significantly.

Federal price controls in the early 1970s re-enforced the practice of automatic seniority increases in billing rates. While government regulations limited across-the-board price increases, increases that resulted from preexisting schedules and practices were permitted. Consequently, regularly scheduled increases in lawyer rates based on years in practice gained the regulatory stamp of approval. After price controls ended in the mid-1970s, firms often increased their rates annually across the board in response to inflation and the market's willingness to bear higher rates. Clients rarely demurred to the increases. The high inflation that occurred in the late seventies and early eighties created an "inflation mentality" that made such increases more acceptable even when they were above the actual rate of inflation. Everyone became accustomed to regular increases in prices.

As firms became accustomed to billing by the hour, billable time became a critical part of each firm's budgeting process and the most useful analytical tool in evaluating a firm's economic prospects and performance. While the starting date varied from firm to firm, by the 1980s most firms had begun to evaluate the contribution of their individual lawyers to their firms based on the hours they had billed and collected. Many lawyers began to confuse their role in selling legal services with selling time. In determining the value of their services to be charged to clients, they began to divorce considerations of quality, efficiency, and results—and to rely solely on the hours invested in the effort.

Over the decades of the 1970s and 1980s, partner compensation grew significantly as a result of increased leverage, increased billing rates, increased billable time requirements, and increases in the time thought appropriate to invest in specific projects. At least from the law firm's point-of-view, the relationship between "value" and "costs" to the client became markedly less important.

PROFITABILITY

By the late 1980s profitability had become the dominant issue for most major business practice firms. For decades information about the relative profitability of one law firm compared to another was largely a matter of rumor and speculation. Firms in the same city did not know for sure how well their partners were doing financially compared to the partners in other firms in town, much less compared to firms located in other parts of the country. The advent of *The American Lawyer's* Profits Per Partner list in 1986 was a veritable opening of Pandora's box for the major business practice law firms and their partners. These reports contained interesting and stimulating information about the size, leverage, revenue, and profitability of the nation's major business practice law firms.

For the first time there was reliable information about the earnings of partners in the largest firms, and every partner in every major business practice firm knew what the competition was able to generate from their law practices. Many partners realized that they could earn a good deal more in a different law firm or in a different law firm environment, and this stimulated their interest in "reforming" their own firms or moving to more profitable ones. The age of innocence in the legal profession had come to an end and nothing has been the same since.

The availability of Profits Per Partner (PPP) information has been a key driver in the transformation of law firms in the United States and worldwide. Firms have recognized that their ability to maintain or increase PPP is a critical factor in their ability to retain their most financially productive partners and to attract new ones from other firms. Reliable profitability information created a basis for comparison against which each of the major firms could be measured and judged in the marketplace for legal talent. At the same time this data has also disclosed to law firm clients how much firms have profited at their expense. In due course most major firms became adept at managing their Profits Per Partner for competitive advantage.[12]

LATERAL MOVES

For decades leading up to the 1970s, the legal profession was stabilized by an aversion to lateral moves by partners and associates among firms despite the long-standing acceptance in the profession that non-compete agreements were unprofessional and unenforceable.[13] Lawyers were slow to realize and capitalize on their status as unlimited free agents. Lateral moves became acceptable during the 1970s: they became respectable in the 1980s, and commonplace in the 1990s.

Lateral moves are occasioned for a variety of reasons including compensation, management differences, personality conflicts, rigid seniority protocols, client conflicts, and the opportunity to establish

---

12 John T. Niehoff, *Take Caution Evaluating Law Firm Profitability*, LAW PRACTICE TODAY, May 2011, http://www.americanbar.org/newsletter/publications/ law_practice_today_home/law_practice_today_archive/may11/take_caution_ evaluating_law_firm_profitability.html.

13 MOD. RULES OF PROF. CONDUCT RULE 5.6 (2007) ("A lawyer shall not participate in offering or making: (a) a partnership, shareholders, operating, employment, or other similar type of agreement that restricts the right of a lawyer to practice after termination of the relationship. . . .). A version of Model Rule 5.6 has been adopted in many states.

greater control of one's destiny. Higher compensation is often the principal issue.

Some senior partners who were unable adjust to the stepped-up pace of the legal practice unintentionally yielded control of their clients to younger partners. As the firms added new clients some clients looked upon the young partners who were responsible for their day-to-day work as their lawyers rather than the senior partners in the firm. These relationships between younger partners and increasingly important clients undermined the traditional partner compensation pyramid based on seniority rather than client allegiance.

Once lateral moves became respectable, many ambitious and hardworking younger partners moved to other firms and took with them the business of some clients. In doing so they usually increased their income and gained the recognition and standing that they had earned by hard work and the careful cultivation of the clients for whom they had worked. Many such relationships did not develop as a result of premeditated plans, but rather as a result of the natural talent and ambition of the younger lawyers and the relative unavailability or complacency of the aging senior partners. There was a growing number of clients that did not have a working relationship with any senior partner, and many senior partners overestimated their role in attracting and retaining the newer firm clients. Senior partners who had grown up in a legal world where they could mentor younger lawyers and "hand-off" clients to them while still reaping the fruits of the relationship felt betrayed by these developments and by their younger partners. That world had ended.

The acceptability of lateral moves also created the opportunity for lawyers to leave established firms to start new ones. In Atlanta, Rogers & Hardin, Long & Aldridge, and Trotter, Bondurant, Griffin, Miller & Hishon were examples of such new firms created during the 1970s.

The acceptability of lateral moves also gave firms desiring to expand their geographical footprint the opportunity to enter new markets by hiring local lawyers to establish regional offices for the new entrants. In the 1980s, major law firms in Cleveland, Ohio led the effort to build national firms with multiple offices. In the late 19th and early 20th centuries, Cleveland's vibrant economy gave rise to several of the United States' largest and most capable firms including Jones Day, Squire Sanders, Baker & Hostetler, Artler & Hadden, and Thompson, Hine & Flory all of which were Am Law 100 firms in 1990. As Cleveland's economic prospects declined, these firms began looking for ways to preserve their prominence by expanding into greener pastures. For example, in 1989 Jones Day acquired by merger Hansel & Post, one of Atlanta's largest business practice firms. During this same time frame Paul Hastings Janofsky & Walker and Hunton & Williams also opened Atlanta offices with the help of former partners in major Atlanta firms. Many of the major business practice firms adopted and repeated this strategy in many regional centers.

OTHER WAYS TO INCREASE PROFITS

Another factor that increased Profits Per Partner during the 1980s was the realization by many major business practice firms that they could increase their charges to clients and in the process their PPP by adding categories of non-lawyer personnel whose services could be billed to clients. Paralegals are the most obvious such category. Now many firms charge clients for a range of services performed by non-lawyer employees with titles such as Case Assistant, Construction Consultant, Contract Administrator, Data Analyst, Director/Manager of Litigation, Docket Clerk, IP Case Assistant, Investigator, Patent Agent, Reference Librarian, Research Project Assistant, and Scientific Advisor.

One example that will be recognized by home purchasers is the use of non-lawyers to prepare documents and close residential real estate loans. These quasi-professional non-lawyer employees manage a large number of complicated documents in a loan closing with the "closing attorney's contribution" being to greet and shake hands with the client. Not so many years ago the closing attorney would have prepared or at least reviewed all of the documents and supervised the closing.

The combination of lawyers capable of creating and editing their own documents on computers, and the performance of more sophisticated support services and less sophisticated legal work by paralegals, permitted firms to reduce the size of their secretarial staffs and increase the percentage of service production activities that were billable to clients. As a result some secretarial time that previously had been unbilled became a part of each lawyer's and each legal assistant's billable time. All major business practice firms have added non-billable administrative personnel to assume responsibility for much of the administrative work previously done by lawyers. Doing so freed up lawyer time that could be billed to clients.

Most corporate law departments vigorously resisted efforts by some law firms to off-load to their clients overhead costs that clients had long expected to be included in the hourly rate, such as weekend heating and air conditioning charges, conference room use, and copy and file clerk time.

A PROFITABLE DECADE

The equity partners of the major business practice firms enjoyed good financial results during the 1980s feeding on the growing size of their firms and the increases in their leverage coupled with the other changes noted in this chapter. By 1985 the average Profits Per

Partner of the Am Law 50 firms had grown to $309,000 as reported in the first *American Lawyer* coverage of PPP released in 1986.[14]

Fueled by the strong economic growth occurring after two early 1980s recessions, average PPP of the top 50 Am Law 100 firms reached $568,000 in 1990,[15] an increase of 84% in a five-year period that experienced inflation of 21%. The prior year, 1989, had been one of the best years financially in the second half of the 20th century for the partners of major business practice law firms. Cravath had the highest PPP of any Am Law 100 firm with average earnings per partner of $1,765,000. The other members of the top five were Wachtell ($1,590,000 PPP), Cahill Gordon ($1,515,000 PPP), Sullivan & Cromwell ($1,210,000 PPP), and Skadden ($1,195,000 PPP).[16]

Heading into the 1990s the major business practice firms were enjoying prosperity without any obvious restraints on the prospect for greater profits in the years ahead. Future growth in PPP would require even higher costs to clients for legal services, a hardship that the clients appeared willing to bear. Continued growth in size, leverage and financial ambition had reshaped and transformed most of the major business practice firms and whetted the appetites of their equity partners for even greater compensation.

---

14 *Catching Up with the Class of '85,* AM. LAW., May 2010, at 102 (providing summary statistics for the 50 firms with the largest gross revenues in fiscal year 1985).

15 *The Am Law 100: Ranked by Gross Revenue,* AM. LAW., July/Aug. 1991, at 16-18 (providing Am Law 100 rankings for the fiscal year 1990); *The Am Law 100: Ranked by Profits Per Partner,* AM. LAW., July/Aug. 1991, at 36-40 (providing PPP data for fiscal year 1990).

16 Steven Brill and Mark Voorhees, *The Twenty-Mile Marathon; The Last Supper,* AM. LAW., July/Aug. 1990, at 6-12,49-50 (providing commentary of the fiscal year 1989); *The Am Law 100: Ranked by Profits Per Partner,* AM. LAW., July/Aug. 1990, at 32-36 (providing PPP data for fiscal year 1989).

.

CHAPTER TWO

The Transformation Continued – 1990 to 2010

T he equity partners of the major business practice firms were in due course copiously rewarded. After a five year hiatus in the growth of Profits Per Partner caused by the early 1990s recession, PPP began to surge again at mid-decade.

GROWTH OF PROFITS PER PARTNER

The following chart reflects the extraordinary growth in profitability enjoyed by the "Top 50" Am Law 100 firms during the 25 year period 1985 to 2010.[17] It also shows the 1985 PPP for such firms adjusted for inflation through 2010.

---

17 At five year intervals the chart reflects the Average Profits Per Partner of the 50 Am Law 100 firms with the highest gross revenues in the year reported. The numbers do not reflect the performance of the same 50 firms at five year intervals although there is considerable continuity in the firms included over the entire

Am Law Top 50 - Average Profits Per Partner, 1985-2010

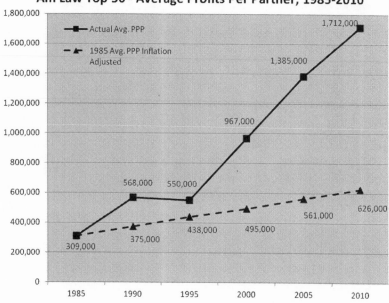

The average Profits Per Partner of the Top 50 firms increased from $309,000 in 1985 to $568,000 in 1990. The United States then experienced an eight-month recession from July 1990 to March 1991 with unemployment peaking at 7.8% in June of 1992. It had been

25year span. The data was collected from the following sources: *Catching Up with the Class of '85*, AM. LAW., May 2010, at 102 (providing summary statistics for the 50 firms with the largest gross revenues in fiscal year 1985); *The Am Law 100: 2010*, AM. LAW., May 2011, at 139-149 (providing 2010 data);*Two More Billion-Dollar Firms: 2005 Gross Revenue*, AM. LAW., May 2006, at 145-46 (providing Am Law 100 rankings for the fiscal year 2005); *Partner Profits Remain Strong: 2005 Profits Per Partner*, AM. LAW., May 2006, at 165-66 (providing PPP data for Am Law 100 in fiscal year 2005); *A Record Year, In Spite of Everything: Gross Revenue*, AM. LAW., July. 2001, at 149-50 (providing Am Law 100 rankings for the fiscal year 2000); *This Year, the Rich Did Not Get Much Richer: Profits Per Partner*, AM. LAW., July. 2001, at 173-74 (providing PPP data for Am Law 100 in fiscal year 2000); *The Am Law 100: Ranked by Gross Revenue*, AM. LAW., July/Aug. 1996, at 35-38 (providing Am Law 100 rankings for the fiscal year 1995); *The Am Law 100: Ranked by Profits Per Partner*, AM. LAW., July/Aug. 1996, at 56-60 (providing PPP data for Am Law 100 in fiscal year 1995); *The Am Law 100: Ranked by Gross Revenue*, AM. LAW., July/Aug. 1991, at 16-18 (providing Am Law 100 rankings for the fiscal year 1990); *The Am Law 100: Ranked by Profits Per Partner*, AM. LAW., July/Aug. 1991, at 36-40 (providing PPP data for fiscal year 1990).

almost eight years since the last recession had ended in November of 1982. The early 1990s' recession temporarily halted the expansion of the major law firms both in size and geographic diversification.

As a result of the recession many of the major firms had more lawyers than they needed, but in expectation of a quick turnaround they did not resort to significant reductions in lawyers or staff. The economic slowdown, coupled with excess capacity, held in check the economic performance of the top firms during the next five years. Average Profits Per Partner of the Am Law Top 50 firms dropped slightly from $568,000 in 1990 to $550,000 in 1995. Because of aggregate inflation during the period, this amounted to an inflation-adjusted decline of average Profits Per Partner of approximately 20%.

However, a new boom in Profits Per Partner started in 1996. Over the next 15 years the profitability of the major business practice firms surged. The PPP of the Top 50 firms increased from $550,000 in 1995 to $967,000 in 2000, an increase of approximately 76%. The boom continued into the new century despite the infamous 9/11 attack in 2001 and the wars in Afghanistan and Iraq. By 2005 the average PPP of the Top 50 firms had reached $1,385,000 (an increase of about 43% since 2000). The PPP of the Top 50 firms continued its upward flight reaching $1,712,000 in 2010, an increase over 2005 of about 24% despite the beginning of the Great Recession in 2007. Between 1995 and 2010 the average Profits Per Partner of the Top 50 firms had increased by 211% during a time when the cost of living in the U.S. had increased 43%.

In 2010 Wachtell Lipton, the smallest firm among the Am Law 100, enjoyed average Profits Per Partner of $4.3 million. Six other firms had an average PPP in excess of $3 million, thirteen others had an average PPP in excess of $2 million, and 47 firms had an average

PPP in excess of $1 million.[18] How and why this great growth in PPP came about is an important focus of this chapter.

CHANGING MAJOR FIRM DYNAMICS

Between 1990 and 2010 the major business practice firms continued to rely on the fundamental strategies that had evolved in the 45 years after World War II. During this period virtually all of the major firms grew in size and most further increased their leverage. However the nature of the leverage had changed; the equity partners no longer relied on "associates" alone to service their clients and to enhance their profitability. New and growing categories of lawyer-employees and billable non-lawyer employees changed the composition of many of the firms and became important contributors to increased financial leverage and partner profits. In 2010 there were 11,926 nonequity partners in the Am law 100 firms. The heavy reliance of many firms on nonequity partners significantly altered the relationships among the lawyers in such firms.

Eighty-one of the Am Law 100 firms in 2010 had at least two classes of "partners." The remaining nineteen had only one. Twelve of these nineteen firms were among the traditional elite headquartered in New York City, three were based in Washington, D.C., and one in Boston. All but two of them reported Profits Per Partner of $1 million or more; eleven of them ranked in the top 20 for PPP.

---

18 *See The Am Law 100:2010*, Am. Law., May 2011, at 139-149 (providing Profits Per Partner and Compensation data for equity partners in each Am Law 100 firm for fiscal year 2010). Profits Per Partner may not present an accurate picture of the relative economic value of partner earnings in different cities because PPP does not take into account cost-of-living differentials among cities.

The National Law Journal ("NLJ") annually publishes a report on the 250 largest law firms in the United States (the "NLJ 250"). Its 2008 report indicated that: "In 1978, the average NLJ 250 firm had 2.5 offices, including its headquarters location. Sixty-seven firms had a single office. In 2008, the average NLJ 250 firm had 10.2 offices; only seven firms had a single office. Thirty years ago, NLJ 250 firms had a total of 84 offices and 567 lawyers in foreign locations. Today the figures have increased to 562 offices and 14,198 lawyers abroad."[19] These changes reflect the growing size and geographical coverage of most of the major business practice firms based in the U.S. and the internationalization of many of them.

Billing rates also increased more than inflation and firms continued to require increased production of billable hours from all of their billable personnel. Two other significant contributors to increased profitability after 1995 were a growing reliance on lateral partners and the increased financialization of the U.S. economy. These changes altered the fundamental dynamics of many major business practice law firms.

LATERAL HIRING

By 1990 most of the major firms had stopped looking for clients among small new businesses with growth potential. Many of them focused instead on increased marketing and promotional efforts to take legal work away from other major firms, and on persuading partners

---

19 William D. Henderson & Leonard Bierman, *An Empirical Analysis of Lateral Lawyer Trends from 2000 to 2007: The Emerging Equilibrium for Corporate Law Firms, Research Paper No. 136,* INDIANA UNIVERSITY MAURER SCHOOL OF LAW-BLOOMINGTON LEGAL STUDIES RESEARCH PAPER SERIES, May 2009, at 1, *available at* http://ssrn.com/abstract=1407051.

in other firms to change firms and bring their clients with them. Lateral hiring became a standard strategy for all but the elite major firms. Lateral partners with significant business often jumped the hierarchical queue at their new firms, complicating the relationships among the existing partners and destabilizing established firms. Years of faithful and competent service were trumped by big books of business new to the firm. Controlling clients' business became the first order of the day.

The lateral movement of lawyers among law firms and corporate law departments has been a principal factor restructuring the major business practice firms and the practice of law over the last 20 years. Many major firms became preoccupied with their Profits Per Partner, not only because of the desire of their partners to increase their own incomes, but also to compete for lateral partners with significant books of highly profitable business.[20] Professors William Henderson and Leonard Bierman have determined that between 2000 and 2007 approximately 11,000 partners left Am Law 200 firms, and approximately 15,500 joined Am Law 200 firms.[21]

The 2006 Am Law rankings disclose that there were 26,949 equity partners and 13,608 nonequity partners in the Am Law 200 firms (an aggregate of 40,557). Consequently, it is fair to assume that during this seven year period of time more than 25% of the partners in Am Law 200 firms left their firms to join other law firms (most of which were other Am Law 200 firms), and more than 33% of the partners in Am Law 200 firms had moved to those firms from other firms (many of which were Am Law 200 firms). Whatever the actual numbers and percentages are, the amount of lateral movement among the top 200 firms has been remarkable and inevitably destabilizing.

---

20 Id. at 3.

21 Id. at 4.

There were a record number of lateral moves in 2009, in part because the market was flooded with partners from firms that had gone out of business including Thacher Proffitt & Wood, Heller Erhman, and WolfBlock. The recession caused the rise and fall of demand in specific practice areas which created opportunities or challenges for the partners affected. In the twelve month period ending on September 30, 2010, some 2,014 partners left or joined Am Law 200 firms compared to 2,775 such moves in 2009. The 2010 number was the lowest since 2000 and "was well off the average of 2,458 partner moves each year from 2005 to 2009."[22]

Wholesale lateral moves have contributed to the failure of a number of major firms including Brobeck, Coudert Brothers, Arter & Hadden, Heller Ehrman, Thacher Proffitt, WolfBlock and Howrey.[23] It is not clear whether partners move because their firm is "failing" or the firm is failing because its partners move, although the end result is the same. The assets of a firm in liquidation (furniture, equipment, accounts receivable) are worth much less in closure than in active operation. Among those injured by such closure are retired partners who have unfunded retirement agreements with their former firm. Growing unfunded retirement commitments are contributing to the instability of some major firms.[24]

The recruiting of lateral partners remains one of the principal operational and financial strategies of most of the major business practice firms. *The American Lawyer's 2011 Survey* of managing

---

22 Victor Li, *Staying Put: The Great Recession Led to a Ten-year Low in Lateral Partner Moves*, AM. LAW., Feb. 1, 2011, *available at* http://www.law.com/jsp/tal/PubArticleTAL.jsp?id=1202479109116.

23 Martha Neil, *Why WolfBlock Didn't Merge to Survive*, ABA JOURNAL: LAW PRACTICE MGMT. (Mar. 24, 2009), http://www.abajournal.com/news/article/why_wolfblock_didnt_merge_to_survive; Brian Baxter, *Adviser: Howrey's End Wasn't Forgone Conclusion*, AM LAW DAILY (March 15, 2011), http://amlawdaily.typepad.com/amlawdaily/2011/03/howrey-gilhuly-cunniff.html.

24 Julie Friedman, *A Heavy Burden*, Am. Law., Mar. 2012, at p.73.

partners, chairs, and other firm leaders of the Am Law 200 firms (120 responded) found that 82% planned to add lateral litigation partners in 2012, 74% planned to add lateral corporate partners, and 57% planned to add intellectual property partners.[25]

In recent years, a number of Am Law 200 firms have merged with other Am Law 200 firms. Examples include the mergers of Atlanta-based Powell Goldstein into Bryan Cave; Long & Aldridge with McKenna; Graham & James and Steel, Hector & Davis into Squire Sanders (one-half of Graham & James' lawyers moved to Greenberg Traurig); Brown & Wood into Sidley; Hale & Dorr with Wilmer Cutler & Pickering; McCutchen Doyle with Bingham Dana; and Piper Rudnick, Gray Cary Ware & Freidenrich and DLA formed DLA Piper.

There were 39 law firm mergers announced in 2010. The two largest involved the merger of major United States based firms with major London based firms: Hogan & Hartson with Lovells to form Hogan & Lovells, and Sonnenschein Nath & Rosenthal with Denton Wilde Sapte to form SNR Denton. One of the first major international mergers had occurred in 2000 with the merger of Rogers & Wells into Clifford Chance. Another important merger in 2011 was that of Kilpatrick Stockton with Townsend & Townsend & Crew to form a 650 lawyer firm under the name Kilpatrick Townsend & Stockton. In contrast, nearly 80% of the 2010 mergers involved the acquisition of firms of 20 or fewer lawyers.[26] The churn continues.

---

25 Alan Cohen, *Building a Breakout Firm*, Am. Law., Dec. 2011, *available at* http://www.law.com/jsp/tal/PubArticleTAL.jsp?id=1202532848173&slreturn=1.

26 Gina Passarella, *Report Suggests 2011 May Be Busy Year for Law Firm Mergers*, Fulton Cnty. Daily Rep., Jan. 10, 2011, at 1.

THE FINANCIALIZATION OF THE U.S. ECONOMY

The term "financialization" is used to refer to the increasing concentration of the gross national product in the financial sector. Although the financial sector of the U.S. economy did not earn more than 16% of domestic corporate profits between 1973 and 1985, this percentage increased to 41% in the decade of the 2000s. Pay in the financial sector rose significantly as well. In 2007 the average compensation in the financial sector was 181% of the average in all other domestic private industries.[27] Financial transactions including mortgage syndications, collateralized debt obligations ("CDOs"), credit default swaps, and synthetic CDOs became a major source of earnings for the big banks, investment banks and insurance companies and, consequently, a great source of profitable new business for the major business practice firms. Multiple and increasingly complex transactions, often involving the repackaging and resale of the same assets, permitted banks and law firms to dip into the same money pot two or more times.

As financial activity and related business became a much larger percentage of our gross national product, the law firms doing this work became much more profitable. The novelty and complexity of this work favored larger firms with specialization in complex financial transactions. The lucrative fees paid on these transactions in effect came out of the deals (therefore from the pockets of investors) and they were a relatively small percentage of the deal (but substantial to the lawyers).

As a result, the banks, investment banks, and insurance companies that were realizing extraordinary profits on these legally intensive

27 Simon Johnson, The Quiet Coup, THE ATLANTIC, May 2009, available at http://www.theatlantic.com/magazine/archive/2009/05/the-quiet-coup/7364/.

and often rushed transactions shared some of the profits with lawyers who helped make these transactions possible. Not only were there many more deals to do, but they were also more profitable to the firms that helped create and document them. Some law firms, like their banking, investment banking and insurance counterparts, milked the financial markets to their great advantage.

DECODING PROFITS PER PARTNER AND LAWYER COMPENSATION

It is important to note that law firms can increase their PPP by manipulating the classification of their partners without an actual increase in dollars paid to their partners.[28] If a number of relatively low paid equity partners were reclassified as nonequity partners, the reported PPP would increase even though the total pool of profits divided among all partners would remain the same. For example, if a firm had profits of $10 million to divide among its 10 partners, it would report PPP of $1 million. Assume that two of the 10 partners earned $2 million each and that the other eight partners each received $750,000. If these eight partners were reclassified as nonequity partners, but continued to receive the same income as before, the firm's reported PPP would increase to $2 million even though the actual earnings of the individual partners remained unchanged. Because of the relative ease of manipulating PPP, the *Compensation—All Partners* chart in the annual *Am Law 100 and 200 Reports* may be a more accurate and useful way of viewing the compensation of a firm's partners.

---

28 See John T. Niehoff, *Take Caution Evaluating Law Firm Profitability*, LAW PRACTICE TODAY, May 2011, http://www.americanbar.org/newsletter/publications/ law_practice_today_home/law_practice_today_archive/may11/take_caution_ evaluating_law_firm_profitability.html.

Because many of the top ranked firms in PPP do not have multiple classes of partners, their numbers and ranking are not affected by their lawyer classifications. However for firms with significant percentages of nonequity partners, their reported PPP and rankings would be significantly affected by including their nonequity partners in the calculations. When nonequity partners are taken into account Quinn Emanuel drops from the number two slot on the PPP chart to number six, Kirkland & Ellis drops from the sixth slot to number twenty, and Boies Schiller drops from tenth to twenty-first; they still have impressive financial results but they are nonetheless lower on the list. Greenberg Traurig would drop from forty-ninth ($1,320,000) to sixty-sixth ($715,000) and DLA Piper from fifty-seventh ($1,135,000) to seventy-fifth ($640,000).

It should also be noted that Profits Per Partner may not present an accurate picture of the relative economic value of partner earnings in different cities because PPP does not take into account cost-of-living differentials among cities. *Law.com* published a report in 2002 comparing the reported PPP of Am Law 200 firms based on adjustments for such cost-of-living differentials.[29] The comparisons suggest that the earnings differentials between New York and most other places in the country are not nearly as great in terms of purchasing power as they would appear based on the PPP reported. The report states that $770,000 earned in Atlanta in 2001 was equivalent to $1,950,000 in New York City. This cost-of-living analysis concluded that only 10 of the 50 highest earning firms in the United States were located in New York City.

---

29   *The Cost of Living: What's the Draw Worth in New York?*, LAW.COM (last accessed Jan. 15, 2012), http://www.law.com/special/professionals/amlaw/amlaw200/amlaw200_ppp_cost-living.html

In 2012, based on easily accessible online cost-of-living comparison calculators,[30] an associate employed in New York City (Manhattan) for $160,000 a year would only need to earn $70,609 in Atlanta to enjoy the same standard of living. Based on median starting salaries and cost-of-living adjustments, a recent report by the National Association of Law Placement concludes that associates in over 40 cities have more real buying power than New York associates.[31]

GROWTH IN THE TOTAL COST OF LEGAL SERVICES

No discussion of changes in the major business practice firms in the U.S. over the last 20 years would be complete without additional consideration of the growth and change in corporate law departments. Chapter Ten is largely devoted to such growth and change. The growing costs of using outside counsel are further addressed in Chapters Eight and Nine.

The growth in size and profitability of the major business practice firms during the last 20 years occurred while corporate law departments were also growing significantly. More recently corporate law departments began to outsource some work to alternative legal service providers—inside and outside the country. Nonetheless, the gross revenues of the Top 50 firms have increased over 1,300% since

---

30 See, e.g., Cost of Living Comparison Calculator, BANKRATE.COM, (last accessed Jan. 15, 2012), http://www.bankrate.com/calculators/savings/moving-cost-of-living-calculator.aspx.

31 Debra Cassens Weiss, Why New York Isn't No. 1: Associates in Dallas Get the Most Bang for Their Buck, ABA JOURNAL (Oct. 27, 2011), http://www.abajournal.com/news/article/why_new_york_isnt_no._1_associates_in_dallas_get_the_most_bang_for_their_bu/.

1985, while average Profits Per Partner of the Top 50 firms increased by approximately 450%.

The increasing costs of both outside counsel and larger corporate law departments resulted in an exceptional growth in the overall costs of legal services for major businesses—more than enough to attract the attention and concern of top management. Many CEOs and CFOs have decided that serious steps had to be taken to rein in legal costs, and they have directed their corporate general counsel to do so.

CHAPTER THREE

Why Working Conditions Have Declined

A s the major business practice firms became more profitable to their lawyers, working conditions for the lawyers
declined. In May of 2005 I participated in the first session
of the *Raise the Bar* colloquium on working conditions in the legal
profession sponsored by the Litigation Section of the American Bar
Association. The subtitle of the colloquium was *A Project of the ABA
Section of Litigation to Reclaim the Soul and Redefine the Bottom Line of
the Legal Profession.*

The colloquium had been assembled because the leadership of
the Litigation Section thought that the lawyer morale problem
had become serious and deserved thoughtful consideration at the
top level of the profession. Brad Brian, a Munger Tolles partner
and Chair-Elect of the Section, was determined to make the *Raise
the Bar* project the signature initiative of his year as Chair. The
program was co-chaired by Yuri Mikulka, a Howrey partner from

Irvine, and Lawrence Fox, a Drinker, Biddle & Reath partner from Philadelphia and an Adjunct Professor at Yale University Law School. Mr. Fox had served as chair of the ABA Standing Committee on Ethics and Professional Responsibility and was the 2007 recipient of the Michael Franck Professional Responsibility Award of the Association. The initial 75 participants were a diverse group of private practice lawyers, corporate counsel, corporate executives, academics, and consultants. A few associates of private practice firms were included.

The project evolved into a year-long examination of working conditions in U.S. law firms with a view toward finding ways to improve them. The *Raise the Bar* colloquium discovered during the year following the initial meeting that:

> First, lawyers at every level complained . . . about the transformation of the legal practice from a *profession* to a *business*. While per partner profit statistics indicated that lawyers have reaped large financial rewards from this transformation, those rewards have come at a price: more hours, less loyalty, increased tension among colleagues, reduced time for pro bono work and public service, and greater disruption of family and personal lives.

> Second, lawyers across the spectrum complained about the reduction in hands-on experiences. Increasing complexity of cases and transactions mean that more lawyers spend more time as parts of teams gathering and sorting information—and less time with clients or in court, arguing motions or trying cases. . . .

Whatever the cause, lawyers are leaving the profession in droves. Others remain in the profession, but are unhappy with their careers and in some cases their lives.[32]

What is to be made of this undercurrent of deep and abiding dissatisfaction among lawyers with the practice of law? I believe that the growth in size of the major law firms in the United States and their increased utilization of leverage are two of the most significant changes that have negatively affected working conditions in the private practice bar. As a result of huge increases in size and leverage the working environment and relationships in most major firms changed significantly, and over time the personal dynamics of these firms bore less and less resemblance to what they had been when many lawyers currently in practice began their careers. I believe that these changes have reduced the quality and increased the cost of legal services to clients.

Other factors contributing to the law practice malaise include increased competition for legal work (and the insecurity that results from such competition), outside counsel's loss of control over the legal work performed for corporate counsel, increasing demands for systematic and standardized solutions to legal problems, increased specialization, and the burden of 24/7 commitments to the practice of law as a result of the communication-technology revolution. The body of the law has grown to such an extent that it is no longer possible for even the brightest and hardest working lawyer to keep current with more than a small part of it.

---

32 Brad D. Brian, *Foreword*, RAISE THE BAR: REAL WORLD SOLUTIONS FOR A TROUBLED PROFESSION, at vii-viii (ABA 2007).

Most of these contributing factors are outside the control of private practice law firms. However decisions about size and leverage are largely within their control. The decision by many major firms to become very large and highly leveraged has had a profoundly negative effect on the firms and on the personal experiences of their lawyers.

Not so long ago throughout the United States most of the largest business practice law firms were very small in comparison to today's firms, and most had fewer associates than partners. Indeed, the largest firm in 1960 was smaller than the smallest firm on the 2009 Am Law 200.[33] The small and amiable professional partnerships of mid-20th century America have become very large and generally impersonal business organizations in the early years of the 21st century.

THE EFFECT OF FIRM SIZE ON WORKING CONDITIONS

For the major business practice firms, gone are the days when every lawyer knew every other lawyer in his firm and most of the staff as well. Indeed, many of us do not know the names of all of our partners these days. Long gone are the days of the "firm family" when every lawyer also knew the spouses, and often the children, of the other lawyers and new lawyers and their spouses were drawn into a tightly knit community of the firm clients, friends and relationships.

As law firms grew in size it was inevitable that major firm lawyers would find it increasingly difficult to know well all the people they

33 In 1960 the largest law firm in America was Shearman, Sterling, & Wright which had 125 lawyers. The smallest law firm on the Am Law 200 in 2009 was Morris, Manning & Martin which had 137 lawyers and $83 million in gross revenue. *Gross Revenue Takes A Fall: 2009 Gross Revenue*, AM. LAW., June 2010, at 95-100; MICHAEL H. TROTTER, PROFIT AND THE PRACTICE OF LAW: WHAT'S HAPPENED TO THE LEGAL PROFESSION 1 (1997).

work with and to take a personal interest in their lives. Because it is very difficult in a firm with a 100 lawyers or more for the firm leaders to know first-hand the professional work and skills of each lawyer, it has become necessary to rely on information that can be easily quantified, standardized and communicated, like hours billed, fees collected, clients attracted, and similar statistical measures. Consequently, the relationship between a firm and its lawyers becomes less personal and more a matter of numbers and reports.

Also over time the prospect of a career-long relationship with one's law firm slipped away. Increased associate leverage meant that the percentage of associates becoming partners was greatly reduced as firms grew. Additionally, the few associates who became partners were much more likely than in the past to see their firm as a way station for a lateral move to an in-house position or to another firm. Most of the firms no longer felt an obligation to support their partners whose careers had been short-circuited by personal or professional accidents or fluctuations in the market for legal services. If market demand for your specialized services declines, you are out of luck and out the door.

Increased numbers also expanded the gap between senior partners and their younger colleagues. As a result of growth most firm managers obtained their view of many of their colleagues from the impressions and words of intermediaries, and through quantifiable information contained in written reports. Most senior partners choose to invest their limited time in lawyers who are likely to remain with the firm in the years ahead. Today, even in the smaller major firms, it is difficult for the more senior partners to develop relationships with any associate. They have to work hard to get to know their partners. Compensation being equal, most associates would rather be part of a firm where they personally know and work with the senior lawyers than one where they do not.

Large size may also increase financial risks. Partners in large firms are more likely to end up on the wrong end of a malpractice suit filed against the firm on account of the work of a partner in a distant city who most of them may not know personally. While the use of limited liability partnerships now shields partners from the misconduct of other partners (unless they themselves are involved in the malpractice, or if they have guaranteed their firm's lease or bank debt), the firm itself can still be decimated, and in the process partners may find their equity and retirement benefits have disappeared. It has become necessary for large firms to put into place procedures and safeguards to protect against rogue partners, or financially distressed ones. In this era of unrestrained lateral moves, a firm with a long history of professional and financial success can rapidly fall apart.

Of course larger firms require more office space, more computers and copying machines, a larger line of credit and more support staff, many of whom are specialized and highly compensated. The decision to add more lawyer-employees is also a decision to add office space, equipment and additional support staff. All the additional overhead must be paid for with even more legal work that the partners must find and supervise. As firms grow larger, the percentage of the revenues generated from the firm's legal work that passes to the partners as profits tends to decline. Increased leverage plays a major role in this decline. In other words, it is necessary to generate substantial additional amounts of legal work just to pay for the leverage and the overhead of larger firms.

Ultimately in large firms some lawyers must supervise the support staff and pass judgment on the new lease and space design, or at least supervise the person who is directly responsible for all of this effort. A lot of lawyers (including some corporate counsel) who signed on to practice law find themselves managing a business. In due course, the need to bring in new clients and to maintain one's production of billable hours generally trumps everything else. However, since the "everything else" does not just go away, it must be added to what is already a long and demanding schedule of billable work and client prospecting. Simply put, a lot more time, effort and money is required to run a "large" firm than a "small" one. Because the number of hours that one person can productively contribute is finite, growth in size has contributed to the extremely demanding working conditions faced by major firm lawyers today.

THE EFFECT OF SPECIALIZATION ON WORKING CONDITIONS

The larger a firm the more quickly a new associate gets assigned to a narrow practice area. Indeed, many associates are recruited by departments of the larger firms rather than by the firms, and in some cases by subgroups of departments so they work only with a few of the firm's senior lawyers if they work with any at all.

Within the departments most lawyers have an area of sub-specialization. Being a corporate finance lawyer or a litigator is no longer enough. You need a more sharply focused area of specialization such as mergers of financial institutions, trials of product liability cases or securities law claims, and many lawyers have an even narrower focus. Senior associates in some smaller firms get a broader range of experience and responsibility than junior partners in some major firms because they are not required to specialize so narrowly.

The significant growth of in-house law departments has greatly changed the nature of the legal services that corporate counsel need from outside counsel. With in-house lawyers providing much of the general counseling of corporate officers and advising their employer-client with respect to its recurring legal issues, outside counsel is normally expected to provide expert knowledge and experience with respect to unusual problems that do not occur every day or about which the in-house staff does not have expert knowledge. As a result, there is increasing demand for experts and decreasing demand for generalists. Many areas of practice that did not appear likely to be taken in-house 40 years ago have been taken in-house. Federal securities law compliance is one such example.

Because of this trend, it is necessary for younger lawyers to develop specialized knowledge earlier in their careers so their firms can justify their billing rates. All of these factors have contributed to the necessity of earlier specialization than in the past.

Such specialization can be a risky business for the individual lawyer. For instance in a recession corporate work usually declines and creditors' rights work usually increases. Lawyers rarely have the breadth of knowledge and the confidence bred of broad experience to be comfortable moving from one area of specialization to another. Consequently, lawyer-employees as well as partners are asked to leave their firms as the markets for legal services ebb and flow and some lawyers cannot be sufficiently utilized to support the firm's PPP objectives.

THE EFFECT OF INCREASED LEVERAGE ON WORKING CONDITIONS

For partners the increase in leverage has both changed the nature of their work and increased the amount of work to be done. As the ratio of associates to partners increased, the number of associates who had to be recruited increased, and the time and attention required in that effort went up while the number of partners involved in the process did not grow at the same pace. If a firm wanted to maintain the same quality of associates, then the time and work required for that effort had to be even greater. Many firms hired non-lawyer personnel to manage substantial parts of their recruiting effort. While this practice has saved partner and associate time for billable work, it has made recruiting the best prospects more difficult, and the strong bond that was often created between the recruiter and the rookie during the recruiting process never develops.

Once associates have been hired, it is necessary to train them and to supervise their work. While there may be some efficiencies of scale, experience tells us that the effort becomes increasingly difficult as leverage increases. Corporate clients sometimes find that associates assigned to their work have not been properly trained for the job, which calls into question the value and costs of the service provided.

It is also more difficult to motivate partners to devote time and effort to the training and development of associates when the odds are very low that associates will remain with the firm as partners or otherwise. Time is too scarce and valuable to waste on a transitory asset. These circumstances can lead to quick assessments of the capabilities of new associates and battles among the partners to control the time of the most talented ones.

When leverage was low, each partner only had to find enough work to keep himself fully occupied plus some additional work to occupy all or part of one associate's time. When leverage is increased by hiring more associates, it becomes necessary for the partners to find additional legal work to usefully occupy and train the expensive new associates that have been hired. It is a tremendous challenge to find and secure large amounts of new business while trying to keep up with rapidly developing law in your field and managing your own practice. Many partners cannot do so and, as a consequence, have seen their positions downgraded to nonequity status or even eliminated.

Many partners prefer practicing law to marketing, but most firms have restricted access to their highest compensation levels to those partners who control the largest books of legal business. That has become the most important determination of qualification for partnership. As a result the importance of marketing has become pervasive. The best marketers are not always the best lawyers. Sadly, it appears that most big firm lawyers now spend more time and give more attention to trying to sell and cross-sell legal services than on improving their legal knowledge and capabilities. Large amounts of time are spent in departmental meetings discussing prospective clients and how they might be lured away from their existing outside legal counsel.

Because solicitation of the clients of other firms was prohibited until the 1970s, law firms used to focus their client development activities on new businesses or on established businesses that required a higher level of expertise than could be provided by their existing counsel. And because the firms could not solicit those businesses requiring such expertise, they relied on intermediaries such as accountants, investment bankers, commercial bankers, and smaller law firms to provide the necessary introductions, or on social and civic relationships developed at social clubs, churches or synagogues, or through other civic activities or family relationships.

The best advertisement was a happy existing client who recommended his law firm to a colleague or friend. As a result, the best recommendation for a firm was the quality of their service to their existing clients. Because the entrepreneurs who started new businesses were more often than not relatively young, younger lawyers often had an advantage in developing such relationships whereas younger lawyers today rarely have such opportunities with the large clients sought by their firms.

Today most major business practice firms have marketing departments and aim their marketing efforts at corporate counsel in an effort to persuade them to abandon their current outside firms and to move their legal business to the soliciting firms. The amount of time and energy devoted to these efforts is quite depressing.

Most small new businesses quickly learn that they cannot use the services of the major business practice firms because they are too expensive and not in tune with the need of small clients for cost-effective legal services. Many major firms will not establish a relationship with a client that does not have the prospect of producing at least several hundred thousand dollars in fees a year for fear of being conflicted out of a big deal because of their involvement with a financially insignificant client.[34] Consequently, many major business practice firms find the representation of small businesses undesirable. Most attorneys do not have the marketing skill set necessary to prosper in such an environment.

Some of the time that in the past a partner would have spent with his or her family, engaged in community affairs, recreating and relaxing, and perhaps meeting and cultivating clients in the natural course of living one's life fully is now used to cultivate existing and potential clients and client referral sources. There is a constant need to acquire more work to support more leverage, including (if you do not generate enough work to keep yourself fully occupied) the cultivation of client-controlling partners in one's own firm. Many lawyers have found these increased responsibilities debilitating. These changes

---

34 DLA Piper is reported to have adopted a strategic plan that requires that any new client accepted must be reasonably expected to produce minimum annual billings of $200,000 or more. Debra Cassens Weiss, *DLA Piper's Strategic Plan Has $200K 'Cover Charge' for New Clients*, ABA JOURNAL (Feb. 7, 2011), *available at* http://www.abajournal.com/news/article/dla_pipers_strategic_plan_has_a_cover_charge_for_new_clients. Many major firms are rumored to have adopted similar policies in recent years.

have transformed the emphasis of many partners from the practice of law to marketing, and to reviewing and editing the work product of other lawyers rather than producing work product themselves.

Many older lawyers have been adversely affected by the growing importance of marketing and the creation of new nonequity lawyer categories (including nonequity partners). This change came about in part in recognition that some partners are much better at finding new business than others. Because the generation of substantial new business is critical to the survival and continued prosperity of large and highly leveraged firms, those partners who can bring in the work have become the equity partners for whom everyone else works, adversely affecting the relationships among the "partners." Some are generous and kind in their relationships with other partners and some are not.

Leverage has also been increased by creating new categories of lawyer-employees and billable non-lawyer personnel, all of whom require the supervision of a seasoned and responsible lawyer. As a result partners are now expected to manage many more people than they were expected to manage years ago. Managing multiple people and projects is much more difficult than managing one or two at a time.

As the number of categories of lawyers at some firms has increased, the level of respect among lawyers in the same firms has diminished. Fifty years ago in most firms any associate who was not on track to become a partner was not permitted to remain for long. Today many firms have "ranks" of permanent "warrant officers" in the form of nonequity partners, senior counsel and counsel as well as several "ranks" of "non-commissioned officers" and "enlisted men" in the form of associates, permanent associates, staff attorneys, and contract attorneys. Many of the more senior of these lawyers who have not been admitted to the partnership are viewed by their partner colleagues (and by associates) as failures, retained for the economic benefits they can bestow and the experienced help they can provide. It's not necessarily a bad life, but it is short on prestige and it certainly doesn't pay as well as being an equity partner. As the competition for existing legal jobs of any sort has increased, most lawyers would rather be employed in such a job than not to be employed at all.

It is interesting that among the most profitable firms, there are a number that appear to have avoided the debilitating effects of multiple classes of lawyers, and have only equity partners and associates. Of the 20 firms in the 2010 Am Law 100 with Profits Per Partner in excess of $2,000,000, only nine had nonequity partners. Five of the nine would have had a PPP of less than $2,000,000 if their nonequity partners were included in the calculation. The PPP of firms like Boies Schiller, which has a high percentage of nonequity partners (55 nonequity vs. 41 equity) reported substantially lower profits per partner than profits per equity partner ($1,565,000 vs. $2,560,000).[35]

For associates higher leverage has been unfortunate in a number of ways; most importantly for almost all it means a diminished opportunity to become a partner. As leverage is increased the opportunity to advance within a firm must ultimately be reduced. It also means that associates will receive less supervision and training. They are also likely to get less meaningful and challenging work, because in most major firms the partners cannot generate enough high quality work to keep everyone happily occupied. Many clients are resisting the assignment of inexperienced associates to their work and refusing to pay for their services.

Large size and high leverage also mean that the associates have less of a personal bond with senior lawyers in their firm. Greater effort by the senior lawyers cannot solve the associate nurture and training

---

35 *See The Am Law 100: 2010*, Am. Law., May 2011, at 139-149 (providing numbers of equity and non-equity partners in each Am Law 100 firm and each firm's Profits Per Partner and Compensation data for fiscal year 2010).

problem because time is an essential and limited ingredient. There is no way a partner can do a better or equally effective job training and supervising two or more associates than he or she could do with only one. Consequently, the supervisor and mentor (if indeed there is anything that could be considered mentoring) of young associates in a highly leveraged firm more often than not will be a slightly older and more experienced associate, not a partner.

A lower-leveraged firm can offer its associates a better working environment. Because the odds are better that an associate with the lower-leveraged firm will remain with the firm, the partners should be not only more able but also more willing to make the effort necessary to train their associates well. Because there are fewer associates to train relative to the number of partners, the partners can more easily accomplish the task and do a better job in the training process. In addition, because there are not a lot of associates available to assist partners, the partners may be more inclined to work with an associate who does not start his or her practice on the right foot. The lower ratio increases the chances that an associate will get challenging work early in his or her career. All of these factors work together to make life in the lower-leveraged firm more attractive for associates.

If you were a new law school graduate, which firm would you rather work for if more than one offered you the same starting salary—a smaller firm with a relatively low leverage ratio, or larger one with a relatively high leverage ratio? To be sure there are a few exceptional larger firms that are growing very rapidly and therefore can also offer better work and a better chance for advancement than other large firms, but such firms are rare among the Am Law 200.

Large and highly leveraged major business practice firms have been a mixed blessing to their partners, their lawyer-employees and other personnel. While lawyers at all levels are much better compensated in real dollars than they were 20 years ago, working conditions have become even more demanding. The necessity of controlling a significant amount of client business in order to prosper within a firm pressures attorneys to pander to the wishes of important clients and undermines their professional independence. The advantage of very high pay has been offset by longer hours, more responsibility, more client pressure, more marketing demands and greater insecurity.

The significant dissatisfaction of private practice lawyers with the profession has grown more significant over the last 20 years. Private practice lawyers have increasingly become narrow specialists dancing to the tune of the corporate counsel who control their destiny. Younger lawyers are getting as much money and experience out of the major firms as they can before moving on to another firm, or to an in-house position, or to a job outside the legal profession.

CHAPTER FOUR

Can Working Conditions Be Improved?

C ould working conditions within the major business practice firms be improved if the firms were smaller and less leveraged? Is there an inherent financial advantage in larger and more leveraged law firms that has caused so many major firms to grow the size and leverage of their firms? Given the many disadvantages of larger and more highly leveraged law firms discussed in the last chapter, why have so many firms opted to become large and highly leveraged? Is large size or high leverage necessary to achieve significant profitability? Is significant profitability the only issue?

The following chart was drawn from the Am Law 200 information for 2009 as released in 2010.[36] It lists the top 20 firms in Profits Per

---

36 *See Gross Revenue Takes A Fall: 2009 Gross Revenue*, AM. LAW., June 2010, at 95-100 (providing size, leverage, and PPP data for Am Law 200 firms in the fiscal year 2009); *Two Firms Fall Below $2 Million: 2009 Profits Per Partner*, AM. LAW. May 2010, at 153-54 (providing size, leverage, and PPP data for Am Law 100 firms in fiscal year 2009).

Partner, their size and their leverage ratios. Added to the top 20 are another 21 firms that were further down on the list with interesting statistics including four Atlanta-based firms. I refer to the chart as the "Lack of Correlation Chart" for reasons that will be apparent.

The ratios of equity partners to lawyer-employees are based on the Am Law 200 information for 2009, using *The American Lawyer* definitions and statistics.[37] The chart also shows the total number of lawyers including equity partners. The method of presenting the leverage ratios shows the number of nonequity lawyer-employees per equity partner.

LACK OF CORRELATION CHART

Firm	Profits Per Partner	Size	Leverage Ratio
Wachtell	$4,300,000	231	1.69 to 1
Quinn Emanuel	$3,130,000	398	4.17 to 1
Sullivan & Cromwell	$2,965,000	700	3.19 to 1
Boies Schiller	$2,880,000	240	6.06 to 1
Cravath	$2,715,000	477	4.18 to 1
Paul Weiss	$2,690,000	653	4.63 to 1
Cahill Gordon	$2,535,000	273	3.63 to 1
Kirkland & Ellis	$2,495,000	1,411	4.23 to 1
Irell & Manella	$2,490,000	199	2.06 to 1
Simpson Thacher	$2,415,000	787	3.45 to 1
Cadwalader	$2,410,000	457	6.49 to 1

37 Equity partners are those who receive no more than half of their income on a fixed basis. *See, e.g., A Guide to Our Methodology*, Am. Law., May 2010, at 123 (defining various terms).

Cleary Gottlieb	$2,385,000	992	4.17 to 1
Weil Gotshal	$2,315,000	1,212	5.59 to 1
Milbank Tweed	$2,230,000	534	3.49 to 1
Skadden	$2,160,000	1,860	3.28 to 1
Schulte Roth	$2,130,000	398	3.68 to 1
Davis Polk	$2,090,000	684	3.05 to 1
Kasowitz Benson	$2,080,000	300	5.67 to 1
Wilkie Farr	$2,005,000	591	3.41 to 1
Dechert	$1,960,000	786	4.28 to 1
Gibson Dunn	$1,910,000	983	2.46 to 1
Latham & Watkins	$1,900,000	1,880	3.23 to 1
Paul Hastings	$1,875,000	917	3.75 to 1
Dewey & LeBoeuf	$1,605,000	1,054	4.86 to 1
White & Case	$1,600,000	1,890	5.80 to 1
Loeb & Loeb	$1,485,000	287	4.63 to 1
Jeffer Mangels	$1,455,000	142	2.23 to 1
King & Spalding	$1,445,000	796	4.09 to 1
Munger Tolles	$1,265,000	180	1.00 to 1
Sheppard Mullin	$1,245,000	479	5.22 to 1
DLA Piper	$1,230,000	1,251	4.87 to 1
Patterson Belknap	$1,215,000	164	2.09 to 1
Covington & Burling	$1,200,000	653	2.12 to 1
Gardere Wynne	$1,180,000	245	2.22 to 1
Williams & Connolly	$1,175,000	236	1.25 to 1
Baker & McKenzie	$ 990,000	3,949	4.48 to 1
Alston & Bird	$ 910,000	820	4.39 to 1
Sutherland	$ 910,000	372	2.61 to 1
Jones Day	$ 765,000	2,469	2.09 to 1
Morris Manning	$ 760,000	137	2.34 to 1
Edwards Angell	$ 640,000	530	5.88 to 1

The chart helps to show that there is no correlation between the size or leverage of the Am Law 200 firms and their average Profits Per Partner.

For example, many of the largest firms in terms of size are not highly ranked in terms of PPP, as the following chart demonstrates:

Size Rank	Firm	# of lawyers	PPP Rank and PPP Amount
1	Baker & McKenzie	3,949	79th $990,000
2	Jones Day	2,469	83rd $765,000
3	White & Case	1,890	26th $1,595,000
4	Latham & Watkins	1,880	22nd $1,900,000
5	Skadden	1,860	13th $2,160,000
6	Greenburg Traurig	1,707	40th $1,310,000
7	K&L Gates	1,705	71st $860,000
8	Mayer Brown	1,657	60th $1,060,000
9	Sidley Austin	1,588	29th $1,460,000
10	Reed Smith	1,427	64th $1,005,000

On the other hand, there are 12 firms on the Lack of Correlation Chart with 300 or fewer lawyers and average PPP ranging from

$640,000 on the low side to $4,300,000 on the high. The smallest firm listed on the 200 list, Morris Manning & Martin based in Atlanta had 137 lawyers, and greater average PPP than 14 firms on the 100 list and an additional 63 firms on the 200 list. Its leverage ratio was 2.34 to 1.

Twenty-one firms on the 2009 Am Law 200 list operated with a leverage ratio between 1.50 to 1 and 2 to 1, included well-known and highly profitable firms like Wachtell ($4,300,000 PPP), Arnold & Porter ($1,010,000), and Stroock & Stroock ($1,065,000). Examples of highly profitable firms in the 2 to 1 to 2.5 to 1 range are numerous.[38] Two notable examples are Kaye Scholer ($1,420,000 PPP) and Gibson Dunn ($1,910,000 PPP). Munger Tolles had PPP of $1,265,000, 180 lawyers and a leverage ratio of 1 to 1.

A comprehensive statistical analysis of all the 2009 Am Law 100 firms demonstrated that there is no statistically significant correlation between number of lawyers and PPP.[39] Larger firms are not necessarily more profitable than smaller firms. There is a weak, positive relationship with statistical significance between leverage and PPP.[40] As a firm increases its leverage, its profits tend to increase, but very gradually. Increasing leverage is a tool that law firms can use to increase profits but it is certainly not the most important variable.

---

38 For example: Wilmer Hale (2.02 leverage) ($1,155,000 PPP); Covington & Burling (2.12) ($1,200,000 PPP); Vinson & Elkins (2.36) ($1,270,000 PPP); Jenner & Block (2.36) ($1,115,000 PPP).

39 A linear, regression analysis revealed that the correlation between number of lawyers and PPP is not statistically significant ($N = 100$, $r = -0.04$., r-squared = 0.002, $p > 0.1$). All the data in the analyses is taken from *Two Firms Fall Below $2 Million: 2009 Profits Per Partner*, AM. LAW., May 2010, at 153-54 (providing size, leverage, and PPP data for Am Law 100 in fiscal year 2009) and *The Efficiency Equation: 2009 Profitability Index*, AM. LAW., May 2010, at 169-70 (providing profit margin data in fiscal 2009).

40 The correlation between leverage and PPP is statistically significant ($N=100$, $r = 0.3$, r-squared = 0.09, $p < 0.01$).

Actually, leverage is an inefficient tool for increasing profits. There is a strong, negative relationship between leverage and profits margins, meaning that profit margins tend to decrease as leverage increases.[41] Firms that achieve high PPP with high leverage must necessarily do so by increasing gross revenues, most likely by charging their clients higher rates or billing more hours, and even then, the gains in PPP are modest due to the smaller profit margins.

It is clear that relatively small firms with relatively low leverage ratios can earn high Profits Per Partner, enjoy high profit margins, create a lot of "Value Per Lawyer" (an *American Lawyer* concept)[42] and perform economically as well as, or better than, most large or medium sized firms. On the 2009 Am Law lists, Wachtell is first in Profits Per Partner, and first in Value Per Lawyer, while being one of the smallest and least leveraged firms in the Am Law 200. It had 231 lawyers and leverage of only 1.69 to 1. Second on the 2009 Value Added list was Irell and Manella with 199 lawyers and leverage of 2.06 to 1. Fifth on the list was Munger Tolles with 180 lawyers and leverage of 1 to 1. Cahill Gordon was in sixth place with 273 lawyers and leverage of 3.63 to 1.[43]

I believe that the proper conclusion to draw from these numbers and comparisons is that firm strategy is far more important than

---

41 Linear regression analysis shows that the correlation between leverage and profit margin is negative and statistically significant. (N =100, r = -0.38, r-squared = 0.14, p<0.001). Profit margin is the ratio of net operating income to gross revenue multiplied by 100. *A Guide to Our Methodology*, AM. LAW., May 2010, at 123.

42 Value per Lawyer is calculated by dividing the compensation to all partners by the total number of lawyers. *A Guide to Our Methodology*, AM. LAW., May 2010, at 123.

43 *See Gross Revenue Takes A Fall: 2009 Gross Revenue*, AM. LAW., June 2010, at 95-100 (providing size, leverage, and size data for Am Law 200 firms in the fiscal year 2009); *Two Firms Fall Below $2 Million: 2009 Profits Per Partner*, AM. LAW., May 2010, at 153-54 (providing size, leverage, and PPP data for Am Law 100 firms in fiscal year 2009).

either size or leverage, and neither large size nor high leverage is a financially successful strategy by itself or combined. An effective strategy requires a plan that differentiates one firm from another in a way that better serves the market in which the firms compete. Unless a firm knows its market and has an effective plan for that market, neither size or leverage will add significant value and either can be a significant liability. There is certainly room for more than one approach, but the advantages for those firms that can operate at the lower end of the size and leverage continuum are substantial.

There are real advantages for the equity partners in these firms. They have fewer young and inexperienced lawyers to recruit, train and supervise. The amount of new business each has to find to support the firm's leverage is less. As a result, more of the partner's working day can be devoted to the practice of law, and less to marketing and administration. Therefore the partners in a smaller, lower-leveraged firm may be able to generate more economic value for their time invested. In addition, the smaller, lower-leveraged firm requires less rent, administrative overhead, and fewer lawyer-employees which should result in a higher percentage of each dollar paid by clients flowing through as partner compensation.

In addition to the financially successful smaller and less-leveraged firms on the Am Law 200 list, I believe there are a substantial number of firms too small to appear on the list that are successfully pursuing a smaller size, lower-leverage strategy. We have several such firms in Atlanta, and I know that some have preferred to stay with their current arrangements and have passed up opportunities to become part of one of the larger firms.

The difference in a leverage ratio of 1 to 1 compared to a ratio of 2 to 1, or 3 to 1 may not sound like much, but the financial and cultural advantages of a lower ratio can be enormous. A firm that is able to generate competitive Profits Per Partner with a lower leverage ratio has a big advantage over more leveraged competitors with the same PPP. These advantages exist in terms of better firm dynamics and culture, more cost-effective service to clients, better intra-firm lawyer relationships, less required marketing efforts, better working conditions, less stress, less administrative cost, less recruiting, and better training for young lawyers.

How can any firm produce average Profits Per Partner of more than $1 million a year with fewer than 250 lawyers and a leverage ratio of less than 2.5 to 1? Seven U.S. firms listed on the Am Law 200 managed to do it in 2009 (Wachtell, Irell & Manella, Jeffer Mangels, Munger Tolles, Patterson Belknap, Gardere Wynne, and Williams & Connolly). Foremost, each of these firms has a superior reputation in one or more critical area of practice. They have used that strength, their superior working conditions and their superior prospects for partnership to attract superior talent, and have then provided high quality training, and a close-knit working environment in which most of the firm's lawyers feel they are working as a team, making a contribution, and being challenged by their work.

Within this sort of law firm working environment, the lawyers at all levels often enjoy working hard and are well paid for the effort. I also suspect that these firms are sought out by clients who have especially challenging problems that require legal advice from established experts with outstanding records of success on behalf of their clients. And such clients are more than willing to pay the price of such counsel.

It is equally clear that small size and low leverage do not constitute a strategy either, and cannot produce high levels of compensation unless they are accompanied by a superior reputation supported by superior capabilities. The financially successful firm must also offer outstanding service, a great record of success in their work, and cutting-edge expertise in areas of practice involving important transactions or disputes that can be of life-and-death importance to their clients. For litigation firms, an unusually strong record of success in the courts or in arbitration is necessary.

Consequently, most firms will not be able to make this smaller sized, lower-leveraged model work with outstanding financial results. It would also be very difficult, financially and culturally, for a firm that has operated as a large highly leveraged firm to survive its conversion to a smaller lower-leveraged firm. Small size and low leverage are not for everybody.

Every firm that is thinking about growing in size and increasing its leverage needs to think seriously about these issues before pursuing such a course of action. Greater size and leverage do not guarantee financial success, and can undermine much that makes the practice of law attractive in the first place. While many smaller firms do not enjoy the same level of financial success as the major firms, they do more than well enough, and their partners and other lawyers find that the totality of their professional and personal lives provides them a better result than a million dollar-plus income in a large and highly leveraged firm. I think that a lot of firms that elected to merge or grow aggressively in size and leverage over the past 15 years will find that their efforts would have been better directed toward improving the quality of their knowledge, personnel, training and practice.

ASSOCIATE WORKING CONDITIONS

Could associate working conditions be improved by reducing their billable hour requirements? Many firms will deny that they have such requirements and some may not, but most do. Regardless of the official policy, associates have noticed that if they do not produce a high number of billable hours, the failure to do so is likely to be attributed to their shortcomings rather than to excesses in their firms' policies.

A survey conducted by *ABA Journal* and published in the February 2007 edition indicated that an overwhelming number of the young lawyers who responded would welcome an opportunity to work fewer hours for less pay. "Of the 2,377 respondents who answered all or part of the survey, 84.2% indicated they would be willing to earn less money in exchange for lower billable-hour requirements . . . . A majority of respondents—no matter how much they wanted to work—were willing to accept a pay cut equal to the percentage reduction in their work load." The survey also indicated that 15.1% of those looking for a 20% cut in billable hours would be willing to sacrifice 25% or 30% of their pay for less time at work.[44]

A similar survey conducted by *The Daily Report* in the Atlanta market in 2007 "showed less willingness to sacrifice pay for more leisure, but 38.6% [of the respondents] indicated that they would have preferred a 10% reduction in minimum billable-hour expectations to the pay raise of approximately 18% instituted by most of the major firms [that year]."[45]

Despite the compelling results of these polls, many major firm leaders and their consultants have concluded that associates are soft and getting worse every year or that it's not possible to be a first rate lawyer without working at least 50 or 60 hours a week. The fact that almost 80% of major law firm associates will leave their firms for other opportunities within five years of their employment apparently doesn't

---

44 Stephanie Francis Ward, *The Ultimate Time-Money Tradeoff*, ABA JOURNAL (Feb. 21, 2007), *available at* http://www.abajournal.com/magazine/article/the_ultimate_time_money_trade_off1/.

45 Michael H. Trotter, *The Higher Pay/More Billables Rush: Firms' Hiring and Promotion Practices Impose Considerable and Unnecessary Costs on Their Clients*, FULTON CNTY. DAILY REPORT, Apr. 5, 2007.

tell the major firms anything they deem relevant about their personnel policies and firm strategies. Moreover, the firms seem to have no awareness of the considerable and unnecessary costs that their hiring and promotion practices impose on their lawyers and their clients.

Recent law graduates also appear to be unaware of the pathology of these policies. Some seem to think that corporate counsel, many of whom work similar hours, should feel sorry for them and demand that their firms reduce their workloads just as corporate counsel have insisted that their firms hire more women and minorities. Unfortunately for the associates, corporate counsel do not appear to have much sympathy for their situation. Many corporate law departments now refuse to pay for first year associate work (and some for second and third year associate work) which is unlikely to encourage the firms to maintain their current pay scales. On the other hand, if the major firms do not hire first year associates it is not clear how they would be trained and prepared for in-house employment.

The insensitivity of associates and partners alike to the needs of clients is not surprising since law schools have generally ignored issues like the cost of legal services, the economics of the practice of law, and the financial and operational relationships that exist between business clients and their major law firms. The Emory University School of Law gave me the opportunity to teach such courses in the early 1990s, but most law schools have been slow to follow suit. An awareness of the importance of these issues to lawyers and for the legal profession is beginning to sink into the consciousness of some law school administrations. In 2004 the Harvard Law School announced its new *Center on Lawyers and the Professional Services Industry*, which billed itself as the only academic enterprise in the country devoted to the empirical study of law and professional services.[46]

---

46 *Program Description*, HARVARD LAW SCHOOL: PROGRAM ON THE LEGAL PROFESSION, http://www.law.harvard.edu/programs/plp/pages/aboutus.php.

A lot of partners confuse hard work with long hours, and assume that associates desiring to work fewer total hours would be unwilling or unable to answer the fire bell when needed. In the early 1960s, many young associates in major Atlanta firms billed less than 1500 hours a year, but they responded to urgent client needs, working holidays, nights and weekends when necessary. It is not the need of the firms' clients that require 2000 plus billable hours a year; it's the financial ambitions of the firms' partners.

What is it about the professions (doctors, lawyers, accountants, consultants, architects, etc.) that makes them all glorify extraordinary hours on the job? Why is it assumed that the only good professional is an overworked professional? At least part of the rationale is that a significant part of what professionals sell is experience, and there is an important relationship between what they have done and what they know. Consequently, the willingness to work long and hard is universally associated with a high level of professional ability and competence.

However, we all recognize that at some point it is better to rest than to continue working. Rest aids mental retention and precision. Reflection can yield insight or a fresh and more effective perspective. Would you prefer that your brain surgeon had a good night's sleep before operating on you, or that he had stayed up all of the preceding night operating on patients in the emergency room? We know that athletes can over-train and lose their competitive edge as a result. The need for down-time in order to maintain peak performance is recognized in many fields, but generally not in major law firms.[47]

I cannot imagine any corporate counsel who would prefer to have a lawyer, even an excellent lawyer, representing her company in

---

47   Debra Cassens Weiss, *Why Lawyers Should Work No More than 40 Hours a Week*, ABA JOURNAL, (Aug. 11, 2010), http://www.abajournal.com/news/article/why_lawyers_should_work_no_more_than_40_hours_a_week.

the courtroom or in a critical negotiation who had been up most of the prior night working on some other client's business. Nor would she be particularly pleased if the lawyer had spent all of the prior night working on her business as a result of not getting started on her business sooner because of commitments to other clients. Who would not prefer the services of an excellent, well-prepared and also well-rested lawyer? Yet law firms habitually sell their clients the services of exhausted lawyers.

Many clients appear to be more aware of these issues than their lawyers think they are. For example, many have policies limiting the number of hours an attorney may bill to their files in a day, or at least a warning flag in their matter management system that helps them monitor longer hours. Most clients also find it a burden when lawyers familiar with their business practices and personnel disappear from their account at regular intervals or completely to work for other clients, or because they have been fired or decided to move to other employment. And then there are the issues of time records padded or nonproductive time charged to maintain revenue levels, or files grazed to meet billing requirements in order to remain employed or to be promoted.

It is not surprising that many big firm partners who entered the profession over the last 30 years think that money is the only viable inducement to students graduating from law school, because many of these partners were highly motivated by money when they chose the profession and the firms they joined. Consequently, law firms that find themselves locked into the model of high pay and high billable requirements are unwilling or unable to figure out how to create a more attractive working environment. Most seem determined to press ahead without an awareness of their strategy (much less to make any effort to find a new one) and hope for the best as long as their practices remain highly profitable. As Richard Susskind, the English legal futurist and commentator, has noted: "It's hard to convince a room full of millionaires that they have their business model wrong."[48]

Make no mistake about it: changing a major firm's direction in the midst of a of hundreds of firms on the same path is like turning around an aircraft carrier, or running against, rather than with, the stampeding bulls at Pamplona. Most lawyers are creatures of precedent and have been educated to follow rather than to lead. As a practical matter most Am Law 200 firms have followed the lead of the major business practice firms in New York City on salary, size and staffing matters for more than a half century.

Is it possible that major firms could be flexible enough to accommodate those of their associates who would prefer less work for less pay? Could major firms continue to attract "top talent" while permitting some of their associates to work less than others for less pay? I think that they could, but it would almost certainly require that the partners make an investment in the firm's future by foregoing some of their profits to finance the change. If changing a firm is going to cost its partners profits, why might they wish to undertake it? Only if doing so is a matter of survival that trumps short-term profits.

Unfortunately, the financial facts of life make this very difficult. Most Am Law 200 firms have built up very large overhead expenses. In Atlanta the major firms have average associate overhead in the range of $200,000 a year, give or take $25,000. The overhead per associate in New York and other of the largest cities is even higher. For most firms only 30% to 50% of each dollar collected in fees translates into dollars for the partners. Assume that a firm's first-year associates are scheduled to earn $140,000 a year and their time will be

---

48 *Keynote Speech on the "Changing Legal Landscape" by Renowned Legal Scholar, Professor Richard Susskind*, Assoc. of Corp. Counsel, (May 17, 2011), http://www.acc.com/aboutacc/newsroom/pressreleases/Changing-Legal-Landscape-As-Viewed-By-Renowned-Prof-Susskind.cfm.

billed to clients at $250 an hour. If the firm were to reduce by 10% its billable hour requirements (i.e. from 2000 to 1800 hours) the firm's revenue would be cut by $50,000 per associate while the overhead remained much the same. As a result it would be necessary to cut the associates' pay by approximately $50,000, or 36%, to $90,000 in order to realize the same profit to the firm from the associates' work after a 10% reduction in billable hours.

This is a result in part of large fixed overhead that is not significantly reduced if associates work fewer hours. By the same token, since overhead is not significantly increased when associates work more hours, it is particularly attractive to law firms to increase the number of billable hours worked by their associates rather than to reduce them.

In short, there is no way that a firm can reduce associate billable hours without some combination of the firm's associates, partners and clients taking a substantial financial hit, and I don't sense any enthusiasm on the part of clients or partners to pick up the tab. While at least some associates appear to be willing to take less money for less work, few if any understand just how much less money they would have to accept to avoid adversely affecting the finances of their firm's partners. It is unlikely that many associates would accept a 36% cut in pay in order to enjoy a 10% reduction in their working hours.

Much of the dissatisfaction with working conditions in the major business practice firms and with service to clients is a result of the very large and highly leveraged model embraced by most of these firms and their appetite for huge incomes. Client service is adversely affected by both size and leverage, and each contributes to the dissatisfaction of lawyers working in such firms.

CHAPTER FIVE

Inside Counsel Frustrations with Outside Counsel

T he crux of clients' dissatisfaction with private practice firms is the high cost of the service provided. It is not the only basis for dissatisfaction but it is the overriding issue. Higher costs are a fundamental by-product of the prevailing major business practice firm model and the desire of major firm partners for very large incomes. Cost is a critical issue that merits two chapters of its own and we will return to it in Chapters Eight: Costs: Part 1—The Associate Compensation Dilemma and Nine: Costs: Part 2—The Costs of Using Outside Counsel. In the meantime we will consider some of the other frustrations of corporate counsel with many outside firms. Greatly increased size and leverage have both had a significant impact on the relationship between private practice firms and the law departments of their clients.

The result of the increasing leverage utilized by most major business practice firms has been to reduce the overall quality of the legal services provided by these law firms and increase their cost. Given that most major firms have leverage ratios of 2 to 1 or higher, two-thirds or more of their work is now done by relatively inexperienced and overpriced lawyers.

What has changed in the nature of the practice of law over the last 50 years that now produces a much higher percentage of the total work that is suitable for such lawyers? How have so many major business practice firms managed to add so many lawyers and work so many of them so long and so hard in light of the growth in the number and size of corporate law departments and the significantly increased use of paralegals both inside and out?

The obvious conclusion is that the way law is practiced at many of the major firms has been re-envisioned to utilize the services of more lawyers with limited experience and qualifications. As some firms changed their style of practice and increased their profits, it was not surprising that others responded in kind. What in an earlier era would have been seen as the over-lawyering of a matter became the standard in more recent times. While many corporate general counsel have been working to restrain what they view as unnecessary legal work, the growing number of law suits against in-house general counsel and risk aversion could have the effect of undermining the cost reduction efforts.[49]

More experienced lawyers perform a higher percentage of the legal work provided by firms with lower leverage, and most experienced lawyers can provide more cost-effective service than less experienced lawyers. More seasoned lawyers are better able to put issues into context and get to the relevant points more quickly. The hourly rate difference between what most firms charge for starting associates and

---

49 Over the past eight years, there have been at least 21 instances in which corporate counsel have been prosecuted or sued for damages with respect to matters involving their employer's business activities. See Seminar Materials of Taylor English Duma LLP, *Professional Responsibilities of the General Counsel: Risks and Liability Protection* (May 10, 2011) (on file with author).

what they charge for their partners is in the range of 2 to 1, or 3 to 1. There are few sophisticated legal issues that a lawyer with significant experience cannot resolve more than two or three times better and more efficiently than a new recruit.

Clients often call on outside counsel when they need an answer, if not immediately, then in a few hours. Clients generally are not interested in having outside firm associates research issues, write long memos to be then edited by more senior lawyers, and then passed on to the client. Many do not have time to read such memos or care to do so. They want good, quick answers to their questions from recognized experts, preferably by phone or e-mail. Inexperienced lawyers are incapable of giving such advice. Clients generally are well served by reduced leverage which results in less use of relatively overpriced associate time and more use of relatively under-priced partner time.

Lower-leveraged firms fit the needs of clients with corporate law departments better than the higher-leveraged model. The law departments of most large and many medium sized companies provide their day-to-day services as well as many more specialized services. Increasingly in-house lawyers use outside counsel for expert advice on particular issues rather than sending entire matters to outside firms.

Consequently it is not surprising that many corporate law departments have become increasingly dissatisfied with the assignment of young associates to their projects at high hourly rates. They expect their law firms to have a reservoir of knowledge on the issues they are hired to address and they want to deal with private practice lawyers who know more about the problems at hand than they know themselves. They do not expect their outside firms to educate themselves at the client's expense. They would prefer to deal with a lawyer and a firm that already know most of the answers they need.

A much lower percentage of today's young lawyers become partners in their firms than was the case 50 years ago. In Atlanta during the 1960s, 80% or more of the associates at the major firms became partners. Today 80% or more do not become partners. As a result, much of a firm's and its clients' investment in training these young lawyers is lost. In the process, the client has paid in dollars and time for a lawyer to become familiar with its business and its legal issues, and then lost the benefit of that investment because of the law firm's internal management and financial policies. The client is then called upon to bear again, at least in part, the cost of educating another young lawyer about its business and its legal issues. Further, firms often do not rely on the same associates for the duration of a matter, much less for a more enduring client relationship, but may churn many associates through a client's legal matters. This is an inefficient process for both clients and law firms.

A reduction in leverage ratios would have one adverse effect on corporate law departments. With fewer young lawyers being trained by the major firms, fewer would be available to bolster in-house legal staffs. Some corporate law departments are beginning to hire a few new lawyers directly from law school and are assuming responsibility for training them.[50]

Bill Jacobs, the retired General Counsel of EMS Technologies, Inc., describes his view of the costs/experience issue in this way:

> When I was hiring outside counsel, I typically aimed at mid-level partners that I believed had the best combination of experience, current hands-on knowledge, and billing rates. I always had a very hard time justifying the most-senior partner rates for the issues I had, where it typically was not self-evident to me that their higher

---

50 Debra Cassens Weiss, *HP Decides to Hire New Law Grads Rather than Law Firm Associates*, ABA JOURNAL (June 21, 2010), http://www.abajournal.com/news/article/hp_opts_for_training_its_own_in-house_lawyers_hires_four_law_grads.

rates were justified by efficiency. On the other hand, the ratio for mid-level partners, compared with those for less-experienced associates, typically made sense to me.[51]

In many situations law firm size is not a significant consideration in the selection of outside counsel by corporate counsel. The issues are largely expertise, costs, capacity, and service. There are occasions when corporate counsel needs help in a particular issue in a particular city or country. It can be helpful to call a lawyer at a firm with whom you have an existing relationship to get help finding in the firm's organization a lawyer in the right place who appears to have the necessary knowledge and contacts. However in very large firms the partners are not likely to know their partners (much less their lawyer-employees) living in distant cities and countries, especially in different areas of practice. When you don't know the names of your partners or their areas of specialization, looking them up on your firm website does not provide much advantage to your client. Corporate counsel can perform such searches themselves. It may be better for corporate counsel to use their own network of contacts among other corporate counsel or referral networks.

Every lawyer and every practice group of large private practice firms is not of equal quality. Corporate counsel want to select the firm and attorneys best suited to do the job rather than be compelled to use lawyers not of their own choosing. Although most private practice firms try assiduously to "cross-sell" the services of their colleagues to their corporate clients, I believe that most corporate counsel would prefer to manage such decisions in their own way.

As already noted, there has been an extraordinary amount of lateral movement among Am Law 200 firms in recent years. For clients lateral moves as well as mergers can result in higher billing

---

51 E-mail messages from William S. Jacobs to author (Dec. 30, 2010, and July 13, 2011) (on file with author).

rates, quality control issues, adjustments to new team members and new client service protocols, and the loss of valued outside lawyers because of conflicts with clients of their new firms. It is likely that such a move will require that some new lawyers be introduced to the client's business and legal issues, whether the client moves its business with the relocating lawyer or stays with its existing firm. The need to educate new lawyers about the client's policies and business is an expense usually borne at least in part by the client. The larger the new firm the more likely conflicts exist or will arise that will require corporate counsel to seek the assistance of another firm. Trying to find another suitable outside lawyer and firm is disruptive, time consuming and distracting. The wholesale lateral movement within the private practice world is a nuisance for corporate counsel.

Robin H. Sangston, now General Counsel of Cox Communications Inc., said in a 2008 interview with *The Daily Report* that when one of the smaller specialty firms used by Cox merged into a very, very big white shoe law firm "their rates went up, their hourly requirements went up, and I started getting marketed." Instead of continuing to call on the firm when it was needed, senior partners began to call her wanting to make presentations for additional services. "With this economy, I would be concerned that they would jack their rates up and end up ruining what had been a good thing."[52]

All of these factors contribute to the growing frustration of corporate counsel with major private practice law firms.[53]

---

52 Katheryn Hayes Tucker, *GCs Worry About Law Firm Mergers: Some Fear Higher Hourly Rates or Loss of Flexibility in Choosing Outside Firms*, FULTON CNTY. DAILY REP., Nov. 18, 2008, at 4.

53 For other dissatisfactions, see Michael C. Ross, *GCs' Pet Peeves*, GC CAL. MAG., (Aug. 13, 2008), *available at* http://www.law.com/jsp/cc/PubArticleCC. jsp?id=1202423727431.

PART II

FIVE DEVELOPMENTS DRIVING CHANGE

CHAPTER SIX

Why the Major Law Firms Continue to Change

O ver the last 20 years there have been five factors that continue to drive change in the major business practice firms and the legal profession. These factors have grown in strength and importance since 1995 and are largely responsible for the legal services industry as we know it today.

The first is the greatly increased supply of capable lawyers and law firms which contributes to the greatly increased competition among legal service providers. Not only do we have hundreds of thousands more lawyers in the United States than we had 15 years ago, but on average today they are smarter and better educated than their predecessors. Many of them are also more ambitious and more motivated by money. They are swelling the ranks of the major business practice firms and corporate counsel, creating new and different kinds of law firms, and entering practice as solo practitioners.

The second factor that has reshaped the legal profession is the high cost of legal services. The much higher compensation of lawyers at all levels of the major business practice firms has been a significant contributor to the increased cost of legal services to clients.

Changes in how legal services are priced have also been a factor. In 1960 most legal services were not priced to clients on an hourly basis. Many clients paid retainers that were usually reviewed annually. Had the work been priced on an hourly basis the costs would have generally exceeded the retainer payment received. For those firms in Atlanta that did charge for some of their time by the hour, an associate was likely to be billed at $20 an hour and a senior partner at $60 an hour. If the 1962 starting associate rate were adjusted for inflation, it would be $149 an hour rather than the starting associate rate of $250 an hour or more that is commonplace today; the senior partners' top rate would be $447 an hour rather than $600 to $800 an hour or more. The *ABA Journal* reported in February of 2011 that several prominent finance partners were billing clients in excess of $1,000 an hour.

Consequently, the hourly rates paid by major business clients on many matters continue to rise. The *Altman Weil Flash Survey: 2011 Law Firms in Transition* reports that: "Ninety-five percent of firms surveyed have increased or plan to increase their billing rates in 2011. The median increase will be 4%—a number that holds across all firm size categories. Additionally, 97% of firms expect their effective realized rate to increase or remain the same in 2011. Although annual rate increases are raising again—from a median 3% reported in the 2010 survey—most firms recognize that rates alone can no longer be relied on to drive profitability."[54]

---

54 Thomas S. Clay & Eric A. Seeger, *2011 Law Firms in Transition: An Altman Weil Flash Survey*, ALTMAN WEIL, INC., at 1.

These two factors—the significantly increased supply of capable lawyers (and of capable law firms) and higher costs—have been interacting with a third significant factor: mature and competent corporate law departments. As legal costs have increased and as legal issues have become ubiquitous in the operation of modern businesses, corporate management has universally concluded that all but the smallest companies require at least one talented lawyer as a full-time employee to oversee corporate legal affairs and to manage the corporation's relationships with other lawyers. In due course it has become obvious that legal needs of businesses would be better and less expensively served if they had not only an in-house general counsel, but also an in-house law department. The growth of these departments in capability, size, responsibility and confidence has been one of the most important factors accelerating the transformation of the legal profession over the last 20 years.

Growing costs have also led corporate counsel to seek less expensive answers to recurring legal problems by seeking standardized and simplified solutions. Such solutions not only reduce direct legal services costs, but they also reduce the amount of non-legal administrative and operational time and costs necessary for the rest of the organization to do its business without costly legal mistakes. These pressures have encouraged the fourth factor: the standardization and commoditization of legal services.

A variety of developments have combined to transform what used to be customized legal services into legal commodities. There is room to differ with respect to the degree of commoditization that has occurred, but most knowledgeable observers have concluded that more than one-half of the legal services provided by most major business practice firms (excepting a few elite firms in highly specialized areas of practice) have become commodities. My own estimate is closer to 75%. Some projects in their entirety are commodity services. However, large and complex projects are more likely to involve a variety of services, some of which will be commodity services and others expert services. Law departments are increasingly likely to disaggregate the expert services from the commoditized ones which they take on themselves or outsource to less expensive service providers.

To the extent that outside counsel is involved in projects, it is likely that more associate time will be devoted to the matter than partner time. Otherwise, why would the private practice firms have two or three times as many associates as they have partners? One thoughtful commentator has suggested that the best way to determine the percentage of commodity legal work performed by outside counsel is to ask partners at significant firms "what percentage of your work could you delegate to a junior, given that the junior was properly trained to do the work with quality? The answers we get are usually upward of 70%. The implications are staggering."[55]

The fifth factor, technology, and in particular communications technology, has also had a profound effect on the practice of law worldwide and on the structure of what we now call the legal services industry. Close proximity to clients was of fundamental importance in 1950 and remained an important consideration into the 1990s, but the development of the Internet, e-mail and video-conferencing have fundamentally altered the way in which lawyers communicate with their clients and other lawyers, and has facilitated competition among legal service providers, not just within the United States, but around the world.

While we sleep it is now possible for lawyers in India to work on U.S. legal projects that otherwise would have been done by U.S. lawyers

---

55 Comment by Patrick J. McKenna, *Standardized Legal Services and Help For Laid-Off Associates*, LAW FIRM STRATEGY AND PRACTICE MANAGEMENT (Nov. 15, 2008), http://www.patrickmckenna.com/defaultviewer.aspx?ID=40383&OPID=40375&sp=yes.

and paralegals at a higher cost, or for U.S. attorneys in rural Iowa or Tennessee to provide legal services at a lower cost than an attorney based in a regional business hub. Some law firms have tried to reap a profit from this phenomenon by treating the outsourced lawyers as their associates or legal staff and billing their clients a significant markup on their services. Many clients now require that outsourced work be billed at cost, while the U.S. lawyers who farm out the work may still held responsible for the results. Often the work could be and is outsourced directly by the client's own law department.

These five factors: the increased number of capable lawyers and law firms, ever higher costs, corporate law departments, commoditization, and technology—and their continuing interaction—have permanently altered the legal services industry. Succeeding chapters will examine each of these factors.

By 2010, despite the Great Recession, many major business firm lawyers were earning far more money in inflation-adjusted dollars than their predecessors had ever dreamed of earning in 1960, or even in 2000. The notoriety of these high profits coupled with higher legal costs is causing business clients to demand from their outside legal counsel the same cost reductions that their other suppliers have come to expect. Consequently there are growing demands, not merely for reductions in the rate of growth of the cost of legal services, but for actual reductions in the total cost of such services.

CHAPTER SEVEN

Competition–An Abundant Supply of Capable Lawyers and Law Firms

T he most significant factor weighing on the profitability of major law firms in the United States is the tremendous increase in competition to provide legal services. Among the factors contributing to such increased competition are: 1) growth in the number and quality of lawyers and law firms, 2) increasing knowledge and skill of corporate law departments as providers and as purchasers of legal services, 3) improvements in communications technology, 4) foreign competition, 5) growth in the number and quality of law schools, and 6) the elimination of most restrictions on the marketing of legal services.

According to *The Lawyer Statistical Report* prepared by the American Bar Foundation for 2000, the number of lawyers in the United States grew from 221,605 in 1951 (one for every 695 persons) to 930,000 in 1995, and then to 1,066,000 lawyers in 2000 (one for every 295 persons).[56] This represents an increase in number of almost 400%, and an increase in the ratio of lawyers to persons of more than 130%. At the end of 2010, the various state bar associations reported an aggregate of 1,225,452 registered and active members of their associations (one lawyer for every 252 residents of the U.S.), a 15% increase over the 10 year period.[57]

About 40,000 students graduated from law school each year since 1995 (an aggregate of approximately 640,000 graduates) and in more recent years the number of graduates has been closer to 45,000 a year.[58] During the same fifteen year period, the number of registered and active members of the state bar associations has increased by 250,366 lawyers. The impact of deaths and retirements, which are an important part of the available job equation, is much more difficult to determine. One reasoned estimate concludes that annually about 19,000 lawyers retire and about 6,000 new lawyer jobs are added creating a total of about 25,000 new jobs for lawyers each year.[59] It is obvious that the supply of law graduates is increasing far more rapidly than the new graduates can be absorbed into the

---

56 Clara N. Carson, *The Lawyer Statistical Report: The U.S. Legal Profession in 2000* (American Bar Foundation, 2004).

57 Am. Bar. Ass'n, *Lawyer Demographics* (2011), http://www.americanbar. org/content/dam/aba/migrated/marketresearch/PublicDocuments/lawyer_ demographics_2011.authcheckdam.pdf; *U.S Census Bureau Announces 2010 Census Population Counts*, U.S CENSUS BUREAU (Dec. 21, 2010). http://2010. census.gov/news/releases/operations/cb10-cn93.html (showing that U.S. population was 308,745,538 in 2010).

58 *Enrollment and Degrees Awarded: 1963-2010 Academic Years*, ABA, http://www.americanbar.org/content/dam/aba/administrative/legal_education_ and_admissions_to_the_bar/stats_1.authcheckdam.pdf (last accessed Jan. 15, 2012).

59 *More Numerical Proof of the Oversupply of Lawyers*, LAWYERS AGAINST THE LAW SCHOOL SCAM (Feb. 23, 2010), http://lawschoolscam.blogspot.com/2010/02/this-kiplingers-article-on-yahoo.html.

profession. There are now many more capable lawyers available than there is legal work for them to do.

Of equal significance, clients now have experienced and discerning buyers of legal services on their side of the table in the form of corporate counsel. The combination of an abundant supply of capable lawyers on one hand, and of sophisticated buyers of legal services on the other, has made significant price competition a reality.

Competition has also increased as a result of improvements in technology, and especially communications technology. It is now possible for any law firm in any city in the United States or for that matter in the English-speaking world to compete for the legal work of most potential large corporate clients in the United States.

Less expensive foreign competition is likely to increase. It was reported to the House of Delegates of the American Bar Association in August 2010 that foreign "[g]overnments were investing in law and legal innovation as an exportable service. China and India have both created transnational law schools in which students are trained in English about U.S. and international law. The school in China even plans to seek ABA accreditation so its graduates can take the bar in any U.S. state" if they meet residency requirements.[60] Some American law firms with offices abroad can now employ foreign nationals trained in American law at substantially lower compensation than their American counterparts to assist in providing legal services to their U.S. based clients.

Not only are there many more lawyers today: for the most part they are smarter and better educated than many of their predecessors. The number of law schools and the number of law students continue

---

60 *Harvard Prof Sees Legal Profession in Turmoil*, ABA JOURNAL (Aug. 9, 2010), http://www.abajournal.com/news/article/harvard_prof_sees_legal_profession_in_turmoil/.

to increase. Twenty-five new law schools have opened since 1990.[61] As a result, the law schools are flooding the market with capable new lawyers.

All applicants to accredited law schools must take the Law School Aptitude Test (LSAT). The number of applicants for admission to law school has grown in recent years and the standards for admission have increased as well. In the 1990s the average number of LSATs taken annually was 124,837. In the 2008-09 academic year 151,398 LSATs were taken.[62] The number of would-be law students taking the test in 2008-09 was three-and-a-half times the number of students who graduated from law school that year. The number of LSATs administered in testing year 2009-10 was 171,514, but the number of tests administered in 2010-11 dropped to 155,050.[63] The number of test takers tells us that there are many more students considering a legal career than are able to gain admission to law school.

The academic requirements for all law schools are high and for the more highly ranked schools amazingly high. For instance, in 2009 the Yale Law School was the number one ranked law school in the United States based on the average undergraduate grade point average. Because of Yale's reputation for very high admission standards only students with outstanding undergraduate records from high-ranking colleges and universities and very high LSAT scores bother to apply. Nevertheless, only 7.3% of this extraordinary applicant pool was admitted in 2009.

---

61 *Enrollment and Degrees Awarded: 1963-2010 Academic Years*, ABA, http://www.americanbar.org/content/dam/aba/administrative/legal_education_ and_admissions_to_the_bar/stats_1.authcheckdam.pdf (last accessed Jan. 15, 2012).

62 *Data: LSATs Administered*, LAW SCHOOL ADMISSION COUNCIL, http://www.lsac.org/ LSACResources/Data/lsats-administered.asp (last accessed Jan. 15, 2012).

63 *Id.*

A perfect score on the Law School Aptitude Test (the "LSAT") is 180. The lowest LSAT score of any student admitted to Yale in 2009 was 170, which is in the 97.5 percentile, meaning that the admitted student with the lowest score had a higher score than 97% of the students who took the test nationwide. The student with the lowest undergraduate grade average admitted to Yale had a 3.77 on a 4.00 system, and most of the students applying had graduated from relatively elite undergraduate colleges.

The lowest score on the LSAT accepted by any one of the 185 law schools using the test in 2008 was 143, which was in the 20th percentile of test-takers; consequently, none of the lowest 20% of test takers were admitted to an accredited law school. Approximately forty percent of all applicants to law school are not admitted to an accredited law school. The admission standards to law school are high and they have been very high for decades. Law school students today are smarter and better educated on the whole than they have ever been.

Another factor that has contributed to the continuing improvement in the quality of new lawyers in the United States is the profession's reputation as a jealous and demanding mistress. Most law firms, including all of the major business practice firms, work their young lawyers, and increasingly their older lawyers, very hard. At many firms associates are expected to bill 2,000 hours a year, which averages 40 hours a week 50 weeks a year; many firms have even higher expectations. In order to produce 40 hours of billable time in a week most lawyers would have to spend more than an additional 10 hours in non-billable administrative, marketing and educational activities. A lawyer's life has become a harder one and anyone choosing to enter the profession must be highly motivated to take on law school with the known reward for success being decades of hard work and long hours in the practice of law.

Yet another factor that should filter out college graduates who are not highly ambitious and motivated to practice law is the high cost of legal education. Most law schools require a three year course of study with annual costs in the range of $40,000 to $50,000 at the private schools for tuition and living expenses, but somewhat lower amounts at most public universities. It is therefore not surprising that many law students borrow to finance their education. Allan Tanenbaum, Chairman of the ABA Commission on the Impact of the Economic Crisis on the Profession and Legal Needs, pointed out in an interview with the *Wall Street Journal* in 2010 that the average law school debt for students was then $100,000, and that in the current job market many "have no foreseeable way to pay that back."[64]

Young people must be highly motivated to become lawyers if they are willing to take on such a burden, and they must work very hard as lawyers to earn sufficient income to repay their school loans. Bankruptcy law does not permit students to discharge their student loan debts, although recent changes may permit some of the obligation to be forgiven if the borrower makes annual payments of 10% of his or her disposable income for a period of 20 years.[65] Only

---

64 Debra Cassens Weiss, As *'Troubling Indicators' Mount for 2010 Law Grads, an ABA Expert Issues a Warning*, ABA Journal (May 6, 2010), http://www.abajournal. com/news/article/as_troubling_indicators_mount_for_2010_law_grads_an_aba_ expert_issues_a_war/; *see also* Lawyers Against the Law School Scam, http:// lawschoolscam.blogspot.com/ (blog reflecting frustration and anger of many law school graduates with the high costs of their legal education and their low odds of finding legal employment sufficient to repay such costs) (last accessed May 30, 2010); Mark Hansen, *ABA President to Boxer – Law Grads Shouldn't be Overshadowed by Overwhelming Debt*, ABA Journal (Apr. 27, 2011), http://www. abajournal.com/news/article/aba_president_to_boxer_law_grads_shouldnt_be_ shadowed_by_overwhelming_debt/; David Segal, *Is Law School a Losing Game?*, N.Y. Times (Jan. 8, 2011), http://www.nytimes.com/2011/01/09/business/09law. html?_r=2&pagewanted=all.

65 *See* 11 U.S.C. 523(a)(8) (providing that educational debt cannot be discharged in bankruptcy except in cases of undue hardship).

the most ambitious students will reasonably conclude that becoming a lawyer is worth the total investment of time and money.

Since 1960 law schools have hitched a ride on the growing compensation of their graduates by increasing their tuition charges substantially in excess of inflation. For example, the tuition at Harvard Law School has increased from $1,250 a year in 1961-62 to $39,325 in 2009-2010, an increase of 3,150% during a period of time in which inflation increased by 817%. In 2011, tuition at the most expensive law school in the country, Cornell University, was $51,150 while room and board, books, and other expenses added an additional $18,600.[66] The large loans necessary for many students to finance these exorbitant costs can be justified only if these young lawyers can find jobs that pay enough to permit them to repay their loans.

The availability of loans to pay most of one's law school expenses has had the desirable effect of opening law school to many candidates who could not otherwise have paid the costs of a legal education. It also made law school possible for many students whose families were reluctant or unable to spend their disposable income on a legal education for their children. Because jobs were generally easy to come by prior to the recent recession, many law school graduates have been able to repay the loans. Unfortunately, times have changed.

Many law students also borrow money to attend college. These loans usually become due for initial payments six months after graduation from college or subsequent postgraduate education (or after dropping out, if a student does not graduate). As a result, college graduates have an incentive to stay in school, particularly if jobs are scarce when they graduate from college. Some choose to attend law school in order to postpone the payment of college loans and in

---

66 *What Are the Priciest Private Law Schools?*, U.S. NEWS AND WORLD REPORT, *available at* http://grad-schools.usnews.rankingsandreviews.com/best-graduate-schools/top-law-schools/private-cost-rankings (last accessed Jan. 15, 2012).

the hope of finding jobs that will pay enough to service both their undergraduate and law school debt.

Because law schools can charge a high tuition and generally have high student-to-faculty ratios, they are often very profitable to their universities which may use the profits from their law schools to support other university programs.[67] Given the surplus of law school graduates, there is the obvious question of whether the large number of existing law schools are there to serve the needs of the students and the legal profession or to provide income for the universities that create them. This is one of the reasons why the number of accredited law schools in the United States has increased over the last 20 years from 175 to 200.[68]

Legal education has the advantage of enhancing analytical and presentation skills that are useful in almost any professional or business occupation. In addition, there is some overlap between graduate business school programs and legal education. Consequently, many law school graduates become businessmen or businesswomen rather than lawyers, or switch later in their careers.[69] Some students pursue joint degree programs in both business and law.

As hard as it is to get into a law school of any sort, and as hard as the course of study is, you would think that law school graduates

---

67 See David Segal, *Is Law School a Losing Game?*, N.Y. TIMES (Jan. 8, 2011), http://www.nytimes.com/2011/01/09/business/09law.html?_r=1&pagewanted=all# ("So much money flows into law schools that law professors are among the highest paid in academia, and law schools that are part of universities often subsidize the money-losing fields of higher education.")

68 *Enrollment and Degrees Awarded: 1963-2010 Academic Years*, ABA, http://www.americanbar.org/content/dam/aba/administrative/legal_education_and_admissions_to_the_bar/stats_1.authcheckdam.pdf (last accessed Jan. 15, 2012).

69 Mark Curriden, *CEO, Esq.: Why Lawyers Are Being Asked to Lead Some of the Nation's Largest Corporations*, ABA JOURNAL, May 1, 2010, http://www.abajournal.com/magazine/article/ceo_esq/. As of that date nine of the *Fortune 50* companies had a lawyer as chief executive.

would automatically be authorized to practice law. To the contrary, after completing law school students must then take and pass a state bar exam before they are admitted to practice. Only 77% of the law school graduates taking the NY State Bar Exam pass it. Only 65% pass the California Bar Exam. Some will take the exam more than once and will pass it on a second or subsequent try. A significant percentage of law students never pass a bar exam which suggests that the bar exam standards are very high, that some law schools have set their admission standards too low, or that the quality of the legal education they provide is deficient.

Becoming a lawyer has not always been as difficult as it is today. In 1931 only 17 states required two years of college education to be admitted to the bar and only 33 states required that students take three years of academic work in law school. Remaining a lawyer used to be easier as well. The first mandatory continuing legal education requirement for lawyers wishing to maintain their certification to practice was adopted by Minnesota in 1975. Most state bar associations now require that lawyers maintain their good standing to practice by taking a specified amount of continuing legal education each year. Those who fail to meet the requirements lose their certification.

The legal profession today is overflowing with smart, ambitious and hard-working lawyers who are motivated and anxious to maximize their earning potential. The contest to deliver legal services is becoming much more competitive because of the greatly increased number and quality of the available lawyers and law firms, and also because of significant improvements in communications technology. This technology makes potential clients everywhere more accessible to law firms anywhere. It has almost eliminated the importance of proximity for a workable attorney-client relationship.

Not only are there more good lawyers and law firms than there are clients, but professional restrictions on the marketing of legal services have largely disappeared. The dedicated "firm client" is largely a thing of the past. As a result, every firm has the opportunity to seek the business of every possible client, and this greatly increases the competitive environment.

All major business practice firms have marketing departments. There are numerous consultants selling marketing advice to these firms. Most large firms have retained public relations advisers to assist them in securing press coverage of their firms and in preparing promotional materials. Social-networking services such as LinkedIn and Facebook are used to expand the reach of law firm marketing programs, and various types of lawyer "ranking" programs are growing in number. There are numerous magazines, newspapers and blogs covering events in the legal profession both on a local and national basis. As finding and keeping profitable new business has become a greater challenge and a growing expense for major firms and their lawyers, the competition for business has become intense. Marketing is not only an important topic of firm and department meetings: it often seems to be the only topic of such meetings.

Most of the potential new clients for major business practice law firms are businesses already represented by other major firms. It has become commonplace for the major firms to pursue the business of companies already represented by their competitors. In the 1960s soliciting the legal work of a potential client represented by another firm was a violation of ethical standards in most states and grounds for censure.

Most general counsel are courted by outside firms more than they care to be. Firms send newsletters, books and pamphlets they have prepared to promote their services, and give free seminars on important developments in the law to which they invite not only their own clients, but also the executives and in-house lawyers of businesses represented by other law firms. There are usually social events at these seminars and the attendees are wined, dined, and pursued. The competition among the major business practice firms for the legal business of major business clients is fierce and unceasing.

There is a big disadvantage to the marketing strategies of most of the major business practice firms. They are primarily interested in the high level work of large businesses that are willing to pay for the big firms' high priced services. Most big firms are not equipped to provide cost-effective service to new and small businesses and do not desire to do so. By abandoning the lower paying work of most new enterprises (an exception is made for major new business start-ups or spin-offs supported by big business and finance), they may be missing out on the important new businesses of the future.

Of course the major firms expect to take this business away from firms that have nurtured these new enterprises if and when they become larger users of legal services. This assumes that the firms that are currently servicing this lower end of the legal market, which includes many of the New Model law firms, will not increase their capabilities or otherwise be able to do the necessary work. I would not bet against them. Most of today's Am Law 200 firms grew their practices in exactly this way. Because of the various factors contributing to commoditization (discussed in Chapter Twelve), the speed with which New Model firms can increase their knowledge base and improve their skills has greatly narrowed the gap between what the major business practice firms already know and what their smart, smaller and more agile competition can master in a short period of time.

For all of these reasons, the number of capable lawyers and firms available to provide legal services to major businesses is growing by the day, as is competition for the work. The strange thing is that many clients appear not to have noticed and continue to pay a higher than necessary price for their outside legal services.

CHAPTER EIGHT

Costs: Part 1—The Associate Compensation Dilemma

Rising associate salaries has for decades been one of the unresolved dilemmas of law firm economics in the United States. The extraordinary run-up of major law firm compensation over the last 50 years seems to have started in the early 1960s with raising associate salaries at the bottom of the compensation pyramid and moved upwards from there. In the process the extremely high salaries of starting lawyers have become the poster child for a compensation system run amok. High compensation expectations at all levels of the major business practice firms (driven in part by constantly rising beginning salaries) have contributed significantly to the rising cost of legal services.

The starting salary for associates in Atlanta in 1960 was $3,600 a year ($26,553 in 2010 dollars) and for associates in New York City was $6,000 ($44,222 in 2010 dollars). Starting salaries in Atlanta reached $145,000 in 2008 and in New York City $160,000.

Several firms in Atlanta rolled back their starting salaries in 2009 by approximately $15,000. Cumulative inflation on the national level between 1960 and 2010 was approximately 637% while starting associate compensation at major business practice firms in Atlanta had increased by approximately 4,000% and in New York City by approximately 2,700%. These increases in starting associate compensation in Atlanta and New York City reflected national trends in major legal services centers.

Prior to the early 1960s, major regional firms had primarily recruited associates from local or regional law schools or from among the children of their friends and other family and business relationships. Law students without connections had to approach the firms on their own.

The Alston firm in Atlanta sent an interviewer to the Harvard Law School for the first time in 1961 and promptly increased its starting salary from $275 a month for unmarried associates and $300 a month for those who were married to $500 a month. It did not take regional firms very long to realize that they would have to increase their compensation to attract top candidates when they began to recruit at the national law schools. As they did so the New York City firms began to increase their own compensation in order to maintain their historic compensation advantage.

Cravath kicked off the associate compensation race in earnest in 1968 when it raised its starting salaries from $10,500 to $15,000. Ever since, virtually every firm in the United States that considers itself a major firm has responded to increases by its competitors in associate compensation by increasing its own starting compensation in proportion, and usually making additional work demands on its associates while further reducing their prospects of becoming equity partners in their firms.

Almost without fail, increases at the starting level precipitated increases up the line for all associates (although perhaps not as much in percentage or amount) and for partners as well.

These remarkable increases in starting salaries during the 1960s were a result initially of the growing demands for legal services and the shortage of lawyers to meet them. Because the need for legal services in the 1940s and 1950s and the rewards for providing them were both unexceptional, the level of compensation had been low.

In Atlanta the major firms had raised their starting salaries from $3,600 a year in 1960 to $14,000 in 1969, an increase of almost 300% in eight years, and there were similar increases by all regional firms intent on competing in the national job market. The pay differential between many of the regional cities and New York City remained close for several years in the early 1970s. Rapidly developing legal markets and competitive pay made it possible for many of the regional firms to compete successfully with the New York firms for top law school graduates, but in the process the compensation and the expectations of young lawyers everywhere increased significantly.

Higher starting salaries had a significant effect on law school enrollment. First-year enrollment in accredited law schools in the United States had declined from 19,532 in 1948 (when enrollment was still swollen by veterans returned from World War II) to 13,111 in 1953. Enrollment then started back up, recovering to 15,607 in 1960. As the demand for, and compensation of, young lawyers increased rapidly during the 1960s, first-year enrollment in law schools surged to 34,289 in 1970. It reached approximately 40,000 in 1976-77 and 43,518 in 2000-01. Since then first year enrollment has averaged 48,133 and reached approximately 52,000 in the 2009-2010 school year.

First Year Law School Enrollment: 1963 to 2010[70]

With the supply of male law school students and recent law graduates interrupted by the Vietnam War, enrollment continued to grow because of a big increase in the number of female students and a big increase in the number of law schools. There were only 2,103 women enrolled in first year classes in the 1969-70 school year—about seven percent of the total enrollment. Five years later female enrollment had increased fourfold to 9,006 (an increase of over 300%). To educate thousands of additional law students, 28 new law schools were created between 1966 and 1976.

First year male law school enrollment peaked in 1971-72 at 31,845 and has never returned to that level. It gradually declined to 22,019 in 2000-01 and had partially rebounded to 27,341 in

---

70 *Enrollment and Degrees Awarded: 1963-2010 Academic Years*, ABA, http://www.americanbar.org/content/dam/aba/administrative/legal_education_ and_admissions_to_the_bar/stats_1.authcheckdam.pdf (last visited Jan. 15, 2012).

2009-10. Female enrollment grew to 24,305 in the class of 2009-10 (47% of total enrollment). In 50 years female enrollment has moved from insignificance to parity with males. Total first year law school enrollment has increased by approximately 230%.

As the need for legal services continued to increase and the supply of male lawyers decreased during the Vietnam War, many of the major firms hired more women in order to have the numbers of lawyers that the growing volume of work required. However, most firms at that time were reluctant to hire female lawyers in proportion to the number of female graduates. They feared that male dominated companies would not accept female lawyers, that females would leave the practice to raise their families, and some lawyers were simply uncomfortable with professional women as equals in their midst.

In the mid-seventies the growing demand for additional lawyers was muted by a serious recession, which reduced some of the pressures on lawyer compensation, and shortage quickly became a problem of the past. During the 1970s starting salaries in Atlanta only increased to $24,000 in 1980, an increase of 71% while inflation, as measured by the Consumer Price Index, had been 98%. As a result some of the gains in real income realized by associates in the late 1960s salary run-up were lost to the unusually high inflation of the 1970s and early 1980s.

Partners at most of the major business practice firms in the early 1970s began to realize that they could not maintain, much less increase, the higher levels of compensation to which they were becoming accustomed unless 1) fewer associates became partners, and 2) the firms maintained or increased the high levels of leverage they had developed naturally during the 1960s. Some partners began to look at new associates as "cannon fodder" rather than as future partners. Working conditions and prospects for younger lawyers at the major firms declined as a result, and the attractiveness of the legal profession as a career for many young people began to decline. The universal response of the major firms was to further increase compensation.

As compensation increased, law schools began to attract more students who were interested in earning substantial incomes and inevitably there was an increase in the number of young lawyers for whom money was a primary motivation for entering the profession. The growth in size and leverage proceeded apace in the seventies and eighties and the major firms attempted to offset these growing disadvantages with ever higher compensation. The result has been a self-sustaining cycle of increasing compensation and increasingly undesirable working conditions. For the most part the major firms have been either unable or unwilling to find a workable solution to this dilemma. The end result has been astonishing high compensation for associates and an equally astonishing turnover rate.

The next major run-up in starting associate salaries occurred in the mid-1980s. Cravath again led the pack with an increase in starting salaries in 1986 from $53,000 to $65,000 – a 22% increase in one year. By 1990 the starting salary in New York reached $83,000. Starting salaries in Atlanta hit $60,000 in 1989. Another recession in the early 1990's reduced the demand for many types of legal services and forced many clients out of business. A number of law firms failed and most slowed their growth or stopped growing, waiting for better times. As a result starting salaries did not increase again until the economy boomed again in the late 1990s.

When the boom arrived the supply of young lawyers with prestigious credentials was again insufficient to meet needs of the major business practice firms and the revived demand for legal services. The shortage was a result in part of small declines in law school enrollment, the decision of many young lawyers to go in-house or leave the profession, and law firm cutbacks in the early 1990s.

Starting salaries at most major Atlanta firms increased from $60,000 in 1990 to $75,000 by 1999. In 2000, major Atlanta firms increased their starting salaries again, this time to $100,000. The $40,000 increase from 1990 to 2000 was a 66% increase during the decade when cost of living had risen only 32%. By 2009 starting salaries in Atlanta had risen to $145,000 and in New York City to $160,000.

The number of persons taking the Law School Aptitude Test (LSAT) had peaked in 1990-91 at 152,685 and declined every year thereafter to only 103,990 in 1997-98, a drop of 32%. The shortage of legal jobs during the early 1990s and the continuation of unattractive working conditions had diminished the attractiveness of the legal profession, and it was clear that interest among college graduates in becoming lawyers had declined. However, as compensation and profitability began to climb after 1995, the number of prospective lawyers taking the LSAT jumped back to the early 1990s level of approximately 150,000 in 2008-09 and, in general, law school applications increased.

As salaries increased the costs of attending law school increased as well. A greatly increased number of law students financed some or all of their legal educations with student loans. They needed high paying jobs if they hoped to pay off their loans and live well.

THE BUBBLE EFFECT

For over 40 years ever-increasing starting salaries for first-year associates has been a staple feature of the major business practice firms. Had starting salaries in Atlanta increased only for inflation after 1960, they would have been $26,500 in 2010. In fact, the starting salary in Atlanta in 2010 was $145,000 at several of the major firms. As starting salaries went up, the compensation expectations of the more senior lawyers rose as well. Because new partners assume additional expenses, their compensation must be higher than their final associate pay to maintain the same cash flow, and most firms compensate their junior partners accordingly. Unless total firm revenues and profits grow, increases in associate and nonequity partner compensation would reduce the compensation of the equity partners. The other option would be to reduce the number of equity partners.

Very well paid associates expect to be very well paid partners. In 1960 the compensation of first-year partners at most of the major Atlanta firms was around $20,000. Adjusted for inflation, first-year partner income would have been the equivalent of approximately $147,500 in 2010. In 1960 the top senior partners in Atlanta earned about $45,000 at some firms and as much as $60,000 at others. The best paid senior partner in town was rumored to have earned about $85,000 that year. These incomes in Atlanta would be comparable to earning in 2010 of between $332,000 and $442,000 for most, and $626,500 for the top earner. Although these are salaries that most Americans can only dream about, they would be far below the incomes actually enjoyed by many major business practice firm equity partners in 2010.

The 1960 senior partner compensation in Atlanta ranged from 12.5 times the starting associate salary to 16.7 times depending on the firm. Because of the run-up of associate starting salaries in Atlanta to $145,000 in 2008 partners earning a $1 million would be earning only 7 times the starting associate salary. With associate salaries at such high levels, the partners who themselves had been very highly paid associates naturally expected to earn a great deal more than associates both in total dollars and in relative amounts.

For decades the starting salaries of most of the major business practice firms located in the same city have been increased in the same amounts at approximately the same time. Law firms with major firm ambitions have considered it an absolute imperative to match the starting salaries of their competitors regardless of the consequences. This has been done to maintain the appearance of being a leading firm in order to attract higher quality law school graduates and to confirm to clients and potential clients that the firm is able to recruit top talent and is a top-tier firm. Some believe that like "great perfumes" or "great whiskey," a law firm cannot be viewed as a great one unless it and its lawyers are very well paid and consequently are very expensive.

For the most part major business practice firms in the United States have attempted to follow essentially the same strategy despite the fact that they do not all enjoy the same strengths of personnel, finances, expertise and clients. Few have chosen to compete for young talent on a basis other than compensation. Many smaller and less leveraged firms that can offer better working conditions nonetheless strive to meet the going rate of the other major firms. Eventually, firms with lower profit margins are faced with the fact that they cannot raise the salaries of their lawyer-employees and increase their PPP at the same time unless they shrink their number of equity partners, or do something differently from their competition. Most firms cannot overtake a leader by following it around the course. After all, most leaders are getting better too. To close the gap, it is necessary to risk a different tack and to select it wisely. Otherwise you just fall further behind. As sailors know, a different tack may pay off, or may leave the risk-taker in a dead calm and out of the race. Major law firms and their partners are not inclined knowingly to take risks.

It is not surprising that most associates are generally oblivious to the impact of increased compensation on the stability and survival of their own firms. Many do not care because they see their first job as a stepping stone to another and are not planning to make a career of their first employment relationship. The transitory nature of the relationship between firms today and their associates inevitably has an impact on the associate's commitment to their firm and the quality of their work.

Clients in general have not shown any enthusiasm for paying higher fees in order to pay 25-year-old lawyers with no experience $130,000 to $160,000 a year. It is hard for seasoned in-house veterans to understand why a lawyer with no experience or expertise should earn close to what they earn themselves. In response, many clients are now refusing to pay anything for the services of first-year associates and some are refusing to pay for second-year and third-year associates. They don't see a benefit in funding a high-flying salary for a young lawyer who is essentially an apprentice.

For reasons set forth in greater detail in the next chapter, extraordinarily high associate salaries have been exerting terminal pressure on some of our oldest and best-established law firms while stimulating the compensation expectations of more seasoned and experienced lawyers. These developments have pushed compensation expectations to unreasonable levels for all of the lawyers working at major business practice firms. Increased associate compensation has undermined profitability at the partner level at some firms. Declining profitability is very difficult to manage in the best of circumstances, and the combination of substantial relative increases in associate compensation with relative decreases in partner compensation is not the best of circumstances in this era of increased mobility. Once a firm begins to unravel, it is very difficult to hold it together (I know this from personal experience) and it has been accomplished in very few cases with major surgery, luck and inspired leadership.

Major business practice firms have shown very little creativity in addressing this issue, and few have developed a professional personnel strategy that would enable them to escape the associate compensation dilemma or to establish reasonable compensation expectations at the partnership level. Those few firms that have been willing to sacrifice some PPP in return for lower leverage, smaller size and better opportunities for their young lawyers may have the best answer. The decision in 2008 by most of America's major law firms to raise their starting salaries for associates to $145,000-$160,000 a year without adjusting their strategy has continued a trend that appears to be an easy road to oblivion for many firms.

CHAPTER NINE

Costs: Part 2—The High Cost of Outside Counsel

There has been an explosive growth in the total costs of legal services to U.S. businesses over the last 25 years. This extraordinary growth is mirrored in the extraordinary growth of the revenues of the major business practice firms following 1985, and in the extraordinary growth of average Profits Per Partner. The following chart overlays the growth of revenues and the growth of Profits Per Partner of the Top 50 firms on the Am Law 100 list with the greatest gross revenues at five year intervals from 1985 to 2010.[71]

---

71 The top 50 firms in PPP vary at each interval based on their placement on the 100 list. Consequently, the numbers do not reflect the performance of the same 50 firms at each interval although a substantial majority of the firms making up the top 50 remained on the list throughout the entire period of time.

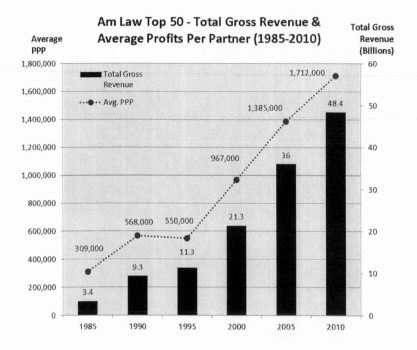

Am Law Top 50 - Total Gross Revenue & Average Profits Per Partner (1985-2010)

The aggregate Gross Revenues of the Top 50 firms increased from $3.4 billion in 1985, to $11.3 billion in 1995, to $36 billion in 2005, and to $48.4 billion in 2010, an increase of almost 1500% during a 25 year period of time during which cumulative inflation had been approximately 100%. Had gross revenues increased at the rate of inflation over these 25 years, the gross revenues of the 50 firms on the 1985 list would be the equivalent of $6.9 billion in 2010.

This extraordinary growth in revenues is even more extraordinary because it occurred while corporate law departments were also growing significantly. In 1997 the 200 largest corporate law departments had approximately 19,400 lawyers. They grew by an additional 8,300 lawyers over the next nine years to a total of 27,700 in 2006 (a growth of approximately 43%). Nonetheless, the total number of lawyers working for Am Law 100 firms grew from 42,600 lawyers in 1997 to 70,100 in 2006 (an increase of 27,500 or about 65%) and at a much faster rate than in-house law departments during the same time period.[72] Some of the major firm growth in size was a result of mergers with other firms. At the same time the major business practice firms and corporate law departments were also hiring large numbers of paralegals who performed some of the work previously done by junior lawyers and secretaries.

The growing costs of internal law departments coupled with the very significant growth in costs of outside counsel resulted in an extraordinary increase in the aggregate costs of legal services for major business clients.

Much of this surge of increased costs occurred between 2000 and 2010 at a time when the country was experiencing significant economic stress. The huge increase in legal services costs for the clients of the major firms went hand in hand with a huge increase in major firm revenues. Indeed, one could not have occurred without the other.

RISING PROFITS PER PARTNER

The average Profits Per Partner of the Top 50 firms increased from $309,000 in 1985 to $568,000 in 1990. After dropping slightly to $550,000 in 1995, they increased to $967,000 in 2000, to $1,385,000 in 2005, and to $1,712,000 in 2010, an increase of 454% over 25 years. Had PPP increased with the rate of inflation over these 25 years, the average PPP of the 50 firms on the 1985 list would be the equivalent of $626,000 in 2010.

The remarkable increases in major firm partner compensation has been and will continue to be bad for private practice firms because

---

72 *Analysis of Legal Profession and Law Firms*, HARVARD LAW SCHOOL: PROGRAM ON THE LEGAL PROFESSION (last accessed Dec. 23, 2011), http://www.law.harvard.edu/programs/plp/pages/statistics.php.

the most important issue they face is the effect of their higher compensation levels on the firms' competitive position vis-à-vis their most important competitors—corporate law departments. The rapid commoditization of many legal services is making it easier and safer for corporate counsel to handle most of the legal work required by their employers, and it would be surprising for them to continue to pay major firm mark-ups for commodity work. The Hildebrandt 2009 Law Department Survey concluded that the cost of using outside counsel is 35% to 50% higher than the "fully-loaded" inside hourly cost per lawyer of $214 an hour.[73]

The publicity accorded the profitability of the major business practice firms cannot help but draw unwelcome attention from the responsible officers and directors of their clients. Much of the high profit at the top of the major firms is drawn from the services provided by the firms' lawyer-employees for whom the clients can substitute additional lawyers working in their own law departments. In the old days clients had to pay for the services of the lawyer-employees in order to enjoy the services of the partner-experts in their law firms. Disaggregation of the services is breaking this profit chain.

From the point-of-view of the major firms, the growth in average PPP over the last ten years has been a remarkable accomplishment, achieved while the country was becalmed in a low-pressure zone of stagnant economic growth and deteriorating economic conditions. Despite the economy, in 2010 sixty-seven firms on the Am Law 100 list had PPP in excess of $1 million. One firm had average PPP of over $4 million, six additional firms had average PPP of over $3 million, 13 had over $2 million, and 47 others had over $1 million.

The average Profits Per Partner and the gross revenues of the Top 50 firms have climbed the same ladder. PPP has grown much

---

73 *Hildebrandt Lunch Briefing: How Does Your Law Department Measure Up?*, HILDEBRANDT, Nov. 11, 2009, at 15.

faster than the rate of inflation. It is no wonder that reducing legal costs and reversing this trend has become a major preoccupation of U.S. businesses and their corporate law departments. The major business practice firms continue to think of "controlling legal costs" as restraining these costs as they continue to rise, while some corporate law departments are thinking of "legal costs control" as stabilizing or reducing the total costs. Some of the efforts to "re-set" or change the relationships between corporate law departments and their outside law firms are addressed in Chapter Ten: The Rise of Corporate Counsel and in Chapter Fifteen: New Model Law Firms.

WHY DO THE COSTS OF LEGAL SERVICES CONTINUE TO INCREASE?

For decades the reasons for increased legal costs included more legislation and regulation every year at every level—local, state, national, and international—the growing novelty and complexity of business transactions (need I do more than mention collateralized debt obligations, credit default swaps, and other derivatives?), increased legal risks to business, the impact of the growing number of lawyers pursuing claims against one another's clients, increased reliance on inexperienced lawyers, overstaffing, excessive research, misuse of modern technology, reliance on the New York practice model, changed negotiating and drafting styles, increased use of litigation and discovery as business management tactics, and hype, hucksterism and hysteria. Most of these are discussed at length in *Profit and the Practice of Law*.

Other factors affecting costs include the increase in multi-jurisdictional transactions involving multiple legal systems and the necessity of utilizing lawyers licensed in different international jurisdictions, the increased size and leverage of many law firms, "performance oversupply" (defined by Professor Clayton Christensen as service attributes above and beyond what clients need), and the financialization of the U.S. and international economies.

In short an increased volume of legal services and higher charges for such services have led to significantly increased aggregate costs for clients and profits for the equity partners of the major firms. Payments based on the number of hours devoted to legal projects rather than on outcomes created an incentive to increase the number of hours billed and to increase the rate of pay for such hours.

The increased use of young and inexperienced lawyers is one of the factors that have significantly contributed to rising costs. Where did all of the work suitable for such lawyers come from? This work did not exist when there were more partners than associates in firms. I do not believe that firms deliberately changed their practice styles and procedures to make use of more associate time; however, as the firms increased their leverage the availability of and need to utilize many more inexperienced lawyers inevitably had the effect of bending the curve toward redefining appropriate levels of research and document review which had the effect of creating more work suitable for these inexperienced lawyers. As leverage and firm size grew, one of the important side effects was increased overhead and higher fees to support the higher overhead. The major business practice firms have become accustomed to carrying a lot of overhead, some of which has nothing to do with the quality of services they provide to their clients, and has a great deal to do with the firms' self-images and their lawyers' sense of entitlement.

BILLING RATES

Steady increases in hourly rates have been a major contributor to the rising costs of legal services. *The National Law Journal* has for many years conducted an annual survey of the billing rates and practices of the 250 largest law firms in the United States. The 2001 survey disclosed that of the 127 firms that responded partners generally billed $200 to $500 an hour, and 14 firms acknowledged a top billing rate of $600 an hour. Most firms reported that most of their revenues were based on hourly charges.

The National Law Journal billing rates survey for 2008 revealed that most partners were billing between $300 and $700 an hour and 80 of the 127 responding firms had a top partner rate in excess of $600 an hour. One confessed to a top hourly rate of $1,260 and another to a top rate of $1,180. Associate rates generally ranged between $200 and $400 an hour. The average firm hourly rate of the reporting firms increased 7.7% in 2007 and an additional 4.3% in 2008. Seventy-one percent of the responding firms raised their billing rates in 2008.

The 2010 version of *The NLJ*'s billing rates survey revealed additional increases:

> The average firmwide billing rate—a combination of associate and partner rates—increased by 2.7% in 2010 .... It's the second straight year of growth rates less than 3%, which is a far cry from the standard 6% to 8% increases from 2004 until 2008 and just slightly higher than the rate of inflation .... The current slide in rate growth started in 2008, when the average firmwide increase was 4.3%, compared to 7.7% in 2007. Growth has slowed even further in the past two years, and the average firmwide billing rate is $385, up just $10 from 2009. Nationwide, among the firms responding to the survey this year and last, the average firmwide billing rate for partners was $470,

up 3% from $456 in 2009. For associates, the average rate was $294, up about 2.5% from $287 in 2009 . . . . Three firms reported top partner hourly billing rates of $1,000 or more, including Foley & Lardner at $1,035; Winston & Strawn at $1,075; and Locke Lord Bissell & Liddell at $1,120. That highest rate was charged by Bryan Goolsby of Locke Lord—the Dallas-based head of the firm's real estate investment trust practice. The average firmwide partner billing rates at each of those firms was much lower, however.[74]

The *ABA Journal* recently reported that several prominent finance partners were billing clients in excess of $1,000 an hour, and Harvey Miller of Weil Gotshal, one of the country's leading bankruptcy lawyers, was quoted as saying: "The underlying principle is if you can get it, get it."[75]

It is important to note that less than one-half of the 250 largest law firms responded to these surveys. I believe that as a general rule the elite firms at the top of the Am Law 100 list do not participate. As a result the reported average billing rates likely understate the true rates.

The *2011 Law Firms in Transition* survey of Altman Weil reported the median raise in billing rates had been 3% in 2010 and 95% of the

---

74 Karen Sloan, *Billing Blues: The New Normal: Billing Rate Increases of 5% or Less: Continued Pricing Pressures from Clients Means Firms are Limited to Modest Yearly Rate Increases*, NAT'L L.J. (Dec. 6, 2010), www.law.com/jsp/nlj/PubArticleNLJ.jsp?id=1202475696179.

75 Debra Cassens Weiss, *More Top Lawyers Break Through $1,000 Hourly Billing Barrier*, ABA JOURNAL (Feb. 23, 2011), http://www.abajournal.com/news/article/more_top_lawyers_break_through_1000_hourly_billing_barrier/.

firms surveyed expected to increase their billing rates in 2011 by a median of 4%.[76]

FINANCIALIZATION

One of the greatest contributors to the environment that has nurtured the rapid rise of PPP has been the great increase in the volume of financial transactions in the U.S. and abroad. Such financialization is reflected in the increased dominance by the finance industry of the sum total of economic activity in the United States and the corresponding reduction in the role of manufacturing, agriculture and trade. Financial activity in the form of the technology bubble of the late 1990s and the housing, securitization, and private equity bubbles of the 2000s contributed to a surge of profit making opportunities for banking and real estate companies and the major business practice law firms that served them.

Simon Johnson, the former Chief Economist of the International Monetary Fund and a professor at the Sloan School of Management at MIT noted in the May 2009 issue of *The Atlantic*:

> From 1973 to 1985, the financial sector never earned more than 16 percent of domestic corporate profits. In 1986, that figure reached 19 percent. In the 1990s, it oscillated between 21 percent and 30 percent, higher than it had ever been in the postwar period. This decade [the 2000s], it reached 41 percent . . . .

76
Thomas Clay & Eric A. Seeger, *2011 Law Firms in Transition: An Altman Weil Flash Survey*, ALTMAN WEIL, INC., at 1.

[The] major commercial and investment banks—and the hedge funds that ran alongside them—were the big beneficiaries of the twin housing and equity-market bubbles of this decade, their profits fed by an ever-increasing volume of transactions founded on a relatively small base of actual physical assets. Each time a loan was sold, packaged, securitized, and resold, banks took their transaction fees, and the hedge funds buying those securities reaped ever-larger fees as their holdings grew.[77]

Professor Johnson omitted one of the big beneficiaries of the bubbles of the 2000s; many of the major business practice law firms in the United States.

Another contributor to higher rates is the trend among the major business practice firms to engage in "performance oversupply." In *The Innovator's Dilemma*, Professor Clayton Christensen notes that: "in their efforts to provide better products than their competitors and earn higher prices and margins, suppliers often 'overshoot' their market. They give customers more than they need or ultimately are willing to pay for." [78]

I believe that the same concept applies to the services provided by law firms. Usually, the fancier and more customized the legal product, the higher the costs to clients. As will be discussed at greater length in Chapter Fifteen: New Model Law Firms, "performance oversupply" has created opportunities for New Model law firms to provide legal services differently, and thus to undermine the dominance of the

---

77 Simon Johnson, *The Quiet Coup*, THE ATLANTIC, May 2009, *available at* http://www.theatlantic.com/magazine/archive/2009/05/the-quiet-coup/7364/.
78 CLAYTON M. CHRISTENSEN, THE INNOVATOR'S DILEMMA, at xix (HarperBusiness 2000).

major business practice firms and their extraordinary Profits Per Partner.

The partners of the major business practice firms take for granted that their compensation should always go up. The managing partner of Perkins Coie was recently quoted as saying: "We want to increase staff and associate salaries in 2011, so we have to increase billing rates modestly to cover those costs."[79] Heaven forbid that the very well paid associates and staff not get a raise this year or that the partners take a moderate reduction in their 2010 PPP of $900,000 to enable the raise! Res ipsa loquitur—let the clients pay more!

THE DAY OF RECKONING

Many lawyers who have reaped the increased PPP benefits resulting from the greatly increased legal fees paid by their clients do not understand how tenuous their situation has become. Naturally, they do not want to accept the fact that the lawyers in-house on the other side of the bargaining table now control the money. With great self-confidence and energy many of the major firms have fought a vigorous counter-offensive. Some have been successful in preserving their PPP produced by the New York Model and others have maintained it by continually enhancing their expertise, and by remaining or becoming relatively small, highly expert legal service providers. Some have done it by shrinking the ranks of their equity partners by "de-equitization," termination, or retirement.[80] Others have manipulated their figures to present a more attractive picture to

---

79 Claire Zillman, *The New Normal*, AM. LAW., Dec. 2010, at 66, 69 (emphasis added).

80 *Id.*

potential lateral partners (while at the same time increasing the risk of adverse client reaction).

Mark Chandler, Cisco's Senior Vice President and General Counsel made the defining statement on the subject in a speech in January of 2007 to the Northwestern School of Law's 34th Annual Securities Regulation Institute.[81] His speech was entitled "Technology in the Law," but it was more about the role of major business practice law firms and the expectations of their major business clients. He noted that his law department, which spent $38 million in 2006 internally and about $80 million on outside counsel, was:

> driven by the same need for productivity improvements as is the rest of the company.... As Cisco gets bigger, the share of revenue devoted to legal expense needs to get smaller. Letters from law firms telling me how much billing rates are going up next year are therefore totally irrelevant to me.... Think about it; not one of the CIOs of your firms expects to get a letter from Cisco explaining how much more our products will cost next year .... So from my perspective, I don't care what billing rates are. I care about productivity and outputs.

Chandler's position is becoming the predominant view of the corporate law department community. More recently it was reported that that:

---

81   Mark Chandler, Gen. Counsel of Cisco Sys., Inc., Address at the Northwestern School of Law Securities Regulation Institute: State of Technology in Law (Jan. 25, 2007), *available at* http://blogs.cisco.com/news/cisco_general_counsel_on_state_of_technology_in_the_law/.

...at an Association of Corporate Counsel roundtable last week there were some words of warning for those firms eager for a quick return to the good old days .... Most lawyers at the discussion ... agreed their budgets would remain flat in coming years. Consequently, many GCs were trying to keep as much work in-house as possible to reduce their external legal spend.

They were also increasing the demands placed on outside counsel no longer willing to settle for the traditional billable hour. Instead, the onus was now on firms to find creative ways to meet these budgetary challenges, whether that involved more detailed value-based negotiations or alternative fee arrangements.

Firms that weren't willing to oblige, most agreed, would find themselves unceremoniously removed from panels.[82]

An Altman Weil survey of corporate general counsel in 2010 revealed that "[c]orporate law departments are increasing their internal budgets, hiring more lawyers and paralegals to staff those departments and decreasing their use of outside counsel."[83] Approximately 63% of the responding law departments expected to spend more internally while another 20.4% expected that their budgets would remain unchanged. On the other hand, over 42% expected to spend less on outside counsel services in 2011 and 27.7%

---

82 *The Lawyer in New York*, May 20, 2010.

83 *2010 Chief Legal Officer Survey: An Altman Weil Flash Survey*, ALTMAN WEIL, INC., at i.

expected such expenditures to remain unchanged. A substantial majority of the law departments expected to increase the size of their departmental work force at all levels.

The corporate general counsel of most U.S. companies face pressure to reduce legal costs and must carefully consider how to get the most value per dollar spent. In order to purchase 2,000 hours of an average associate's time from a major business practice firm in 2011, a general counsel would spend approximately $600,000 (2,000 hours at $300 an hour). For that same amount it is likely that a general counsel could hire at least one and probably two highly trained in-house lawyers with 7 to 15 years experience.[84] These are the economic realities general counsel face when deciding to purchase outside legal services, and that law firms face in marketing their services to corporate law departments. Not paying the outside firms' markup on the services provided by their lawyer-employees is one of the principal advantages of corporate law departments.

Of course, the cost to a corporate law department of using the services of the associate at the private practice firm isn't limited to the costs of the associate. No responsible firm is going to let the associate's work product go out the door unless it has been reviewed and edited by a senior lawyer who will also bill the client for his services.

While there is much said about alternative fee arrangements they can be exercises in mutual delusion. Outside firms hope to maintain or even improve the economic benefits of their deals. Corporate counsel expect to end up paying less for better service. Alternative fee arrangements can provide private practice firms with the opportunity

---

84 The Hilderbrandt 2009 Law Department Survey concludes that the cost of using outside counsel is 35 to 50% higher than the "fully-loaded" inside hourly cost per lawyer of $214 an hour. PowerPoint Presentation from Hildebrandt, *Hildebrandt Lunch Briefing: How Does Your Law Department Measure Up?*, at 15 (Nov. 11, 2009) (on file with author).

to learn to be more efficient and effective legal service providers if they are committed to learning from the experience instead of focusing on their hourly rate matters or measuring the financial results of each matter by the firm's effective average hourly return.

WHY DO CORPORATE COUNSEL CONTINUE TO ACQUIESCE IN HIGHER LEGAL CHARGES?

General counsel are responsible for managing the legal affairs of their company at a reasonable cost. I've thought long and hard about why corporate general counsel have been so accommodating to the major business practice firms and other private practice lawyers when it comes to fees. There is a variety of reasons.

Most general counsel have grown and developed their professional lives based on their skills as successful lawyers in private practice firms, not on their skills as managers. Most have been selected to serve based on their legal skills and acumen. Lawyers inside (as well as outside) have been trained in law school and by their firms to practice law, and most of them prefer doing so to negotiating fees and judging beauty contests among outside firms. Some lawyers have studied business as undergraduates or have gotten a MBA, but most have not. Haggling over "business issues" like fees and legal service protocols with other lawyers is not what they went to law school to do. As a result many law department (and law firm) leaders do not like the management side of their practice. Law department management (or law firm management) is seen as less important than the practice of law: a responsibility that can be farmed out to not-so-good lawyers or non-lawyer executives, but never the other way around. Consequently, most law department leaders think of themselves first as excellent lawyers who nurture and develop their legal skills and those of the organizations that they lead.

Many corporate general counsel learned the practice of law in the sort of firms that represent their companies, and some in the firms that actually represent their companies. The culture within these firms generally affirmed the appropriateness of raising rates every year in response to inflation and the firms' financial expectations. Having learned their trade while practicing law at such firms, many corporate counsel have bought into this conceit. In their formative years they learn that the most important measure of their worth is the billable hours they log, and they receive little or no training in managing lawyers and legal issues. They are habituated to the billable hour, and this attitude often moves in-house with them.

In many cases, they also have continuing personal friendships with lawyers in their former firms and some may hope to return to their former firms or similar ones should their corporate tenure end. Their former colleagues in private practice work hard to preserve these friendships.

One way many corporate legal departments have undertaken to rein in the hourly rates of their outside firms has been to require such firms to affirmatively represent that the client is receiving the benefit of the firm's most preferred rates.[85] In the past some firms appear to have made such representations while disregarding inconsistent rates they have billed to clients. Corporate counsel now have the resources and information technology to check for themselves the rates that large firms and their individual lawyers charge to their

---

85 *See, e.g.*, Wal-Mart Stores, Inc., *Outside Counsel Guidelines*, Ass'n Corp. Couns. (June 1, 2007), http://www.acc.com/advocacy/valuechallenge/toolkit/loader.cfm?csModule=security/getfile&pageid=40433&title=Wal-Mart%20Outside%20Counsel%20Guidelines.

various clients in order to determine if their law firms are living up to their representations.[86]

I would not be surprised to see in the near future some large companies putting their law departments under the management of non-lawyer executives, or at least assigning a non-lawyer financial and administrative officer to oversee the operations of their law departments. It is very difficult for the general counsel to effectively oversee the legal as well as financial and administrative sides of their departments. Pepper Hamilton, an Am Law 100 firm based in Philadelphia, recently announced that it had hired a non-lawyer to serve as its chief executive officer. The new CEO will be responsible for both the firm's business strategy and operations.[87] If a major business practice firm can function with non-lawyer CEOs, corporate law departments can as well.

The Holy Grail of the major business practice firms has been to find a way to maintain or increase the current level of Profits Per Partner while maintaining or reducing the costs of legal services to clients. While everyone would like to think that there is some magical way to maintain the recent extraordinary PPP levels while lowering

---

86 For instance, the *Valeo Partners – Law Firm Database* tracks the actual billing rates 350 firms (including a number of prominent international firms) by practice area and/or position as well as the rates of individual attorneys within such firms identified by their clients, which permit corporate clients to determine if they are in fact receiving the best rate offered by their various outside firms. The 2010 Real Rate Report, a study conducted by CT TyMetrix and Corporate Executive Board "analyzes legal spend from invoices 4,000 law firms submitted to corporate legal departments of various sizes and industries. The study examines $4.1 billion in invoices from 50,000 individual billers across nine different practice areas in 51 metropolitan areas from 2007 to 2009 . . . . By analyzing the billing data . . . . the upcoming report reveals 'how different matter types are being staffed by law firms, what partner time is allocated to a specific type of matter, along with associate and paralegal time, and the overall cost and duration of certain matter types and phases.' " Michael Kozubek, *2010 Real Rate Report Brews Controversy*, INSIDE COUNSEL (Aug. 1, 2010), http://www.insidecounsel.com/2010/08/01/2010-real-rate-report-brews-controversy.

87 Gina Passarella, *Pepper Hamilton Hires Non-lawyer CEO*, FULTON CNTY. DAILY REP., Feb. 8, 2012, at 8.

costs to clients, I believe the only way it can be accomplished is to further increase the number and percentage of nonequity partners and counsel while shrinking the coveted equity partner category to a happy few. It is possible to both reduce client costs and for lawyers to earn very respectable incomes, but there is no way to maintain the extraordinarily high level of PPP for thousands of equity partners in hundreds of major firms at the same time.

Major firms with the very highest levels of expertise will survive and prosper with high profit margins because they will be needed for the most difficult and challenging work, but those below that level are not going to be able to maintain their rates for commodity work because it can be done just as well, less expensively, and more conveniently in-house. Frankly, I thought the effects of continuing out-sized pay increases would have been felt long before the Great Recession.

If the $3.4 billion of gross revenues received by the top 50 firms in 1985 were adjusted for inflation to 2010 the resulting number would be $6.89 billion rather than the $48.4 actually paid to the Top 50 firms in 2010. It is important to remember that the $41.5 billion increase above the effects of inflation that is reflected in the gross revenues of the Top 50 firms in 2010 does not include the billions of dollars that businesses have also spent hiring more in-house lawyers and building their own law departments.

Faced with huge increases in both in-house and outside firm legal costs, most of the large companies in the United States have concluded that they had to gain greater control over the legal aspects of their businesses, both because of growing costs and because of the growing importance of legal issues to the success of their enterprises. They are continuing to do so by increasing the size and improving the quality of their corporate law departments and insisting that their general counsel reduce the cost of using private practice law firms. Corporate counsel have the power and the opportunity to force legal service pricing down significantly, and most have orders from their CEOs and CFOs to do so. I know they can, and I think they will.

CHAPTER TEN

The Rise of Corporate Counsel

T he number, size and capability of corporate law departments have grown with the tidal wave of legal costs. In 1960 only a few companies had in-house legal staff. Many of those that did had a lawyer called their general counsel who was not really their chief legal officer. Some of the in-house lawyers were only middlemen who coordinated the relationship between their company's outside counsel (often "the general counsel") and the company's officers and employees. Frequently their CEO and/or CFO dealt directly with outside counsel without their involvement. Such in-house general counsel often relied on outside legal counsel to sniff out the company's legal questions and answer them.

None of the companies for which Atlanta's Alston firm was principal legal counsel in the 1960s had an in-house lawyer, much less an inside general counsel or law department. The Alston firm provided most of the legal services that its principal clients required, perhaps bringing in special counsel on rare occasions. Major local companies usually called upon a senior partner of one of the major firms to serve as their senior legal adviser and counsel. Senior partners in the Alston firm held such positions with companies such as Genuine Parts Company, Magic Chef, Inc., Gold Kist, and The Citizens and Southern National Bank (then the largest bank in the southeastern United States). Often such senior partners also served on the client's board of directors and perhaps on its executive committee. A few major Atlanta companies such as The Coca-Cola Company and Southern Bell had small legal departments and a real in-house general counsel, but they were exceptions to the rule.

In the 1970s some businesses that had relied entirely on outside counsel began to employ one or two corporate counsel (but not necessarily titled "general counsel"), and many companies that already had a small in-house legal staff began to grow their in-house departments and to upgrade the status of their in-house lawyers.

There were advantages to having a lawyer who worked exclusively on the company's affairs and who was housed with other company executives. In-house counsel was more likely to have a comprehensive understanding of the company's business because of greater exposure to personnel and business operations. The in-house lawyer was also more likely to be available without conflicting demands on his or her time and attention.

During the 1980s the percentage of companies with in-house lawyers and law departments continued to increase; the size of in-house staffs grew as well. In-house lawyers began doing more of the work previously performed by outside counsel. Initially this work tended to be routine matters such as preparation of corporate minutes, qualifications to do business and recurring operational issues such as, in the case of a bank, small loans and questions concerning checks and garnishments. As the in-house departments grew, they expanded their areas of responsibility and thereby reduced the work for which outside counsel was required. Corporate general counsel evolved into a new role as the principal lawyer for their employers responsible for asking the right legal questions, as well as finding the right legal answers themselves or through other lawyers working under their direction (inside or outside). Today virtually all the general counsel jobs are held by corporate counsel.

There was a professional bias in the legal profession against in-house lawyers through the 1970s. For instance, in Atlanta:

> Lawyers working as in-house counsel were deemed a strange breed for many years. The Atlanta Bar Association did not recognized them as "practicing" lawyers and put them in a special "associate" membership category. In-house counsel for several large companies countered by forming the Corporation Counsel Association of Greater Atlanta, which eventually was brought into the Atlanta bar as its corporate counsel section.[88]

As the numbers and importance of corporate counsel increased, many in-house general counsel were frustrated with their treatment by the private practice bar and the absence of support from the organized bar for their role in the legal system. While several American Bar Association committees attempted to address some corporate practice issues, none was populated with in-house lawyers.

---

88 Lea Agnew & Jo Ann Haden-Miller, Atlanta and Its Lawyers: A Century of Vision, 1888-1988, at 91 (Atlanta Bar Ass'n, Inc. 1988).

As a result in 1981 Robert S. Banks, the General Counsel of Xerox Corporation, hosted a luncheon for eight of his in-house compatriots including the general counsel of the U.S. Chamber of Commerce; Sears, Roebuck & Co.; Arthur Young & Company; Aetna Life & Casualty; Sun Company; Texaco; United Technologies; and the managing attorney for IBM. In 1982 the American Corporate Counsel Association ("ACCA") was born with 2,400 in-house lawyers as members. In 2003 the ACCA changed its name to the Association of Corporate Counsel ("ACC") in recognition of its members in more than 70 countries and the global interests of their employer-clients.[89] Today there are more than 29,000 members of the ACC employed by over 10,000 organizations worldwide.[90]

One of my colleagues, who was a senior corporate partner of a prominent Atlanta firm that did a lot of work for a large international company headquartered there, tells of inviting the client's general counsel in the mid-1980s to make a presentation to the firm's corporate lawyers about how they might better serve the company. The firm's lawyers were shocked with the general counsel opened his remarks by saying "You need to understand I am your firm's worst enemy, as I intend to take all work inside to the maximum extent that I can." He then elaborated that he viewed the volume of work in a major law department as rising and falling in such a way that it might be graphed as a sine curve and that he intended to staff inside up to the bottom of the sine curve (but not more so that he didn't have lawyers with idle time).

It followed that he would seek outside help for overflow work above the basic staffing level. Setting aside litigation for which he

---

89 *History of ACC*, Ass'n Corp. Couns., http://www.acc.com/aboutacc/history/index.cfm (last visited Jan. 15, 2012).

90 *About ACC*, Ass'n corp. Couns., http://www.acc.com/aboutacc/index.cfm. (last visited Jan. 15, 2012).

normally went outside for geographic and other reasons, he said there were only two other reasons he might seek help "outside." The first was work requiring a high level of expertise where the company did not have sufficient volume to justify having a full-time staff lawyer with the requisite knowledge and experience, and second was a matter or legal question so important or sensitive that he wanted to be able to assure management that his opinion had been confirmed by highly reputable outside counsel. He reiterated that all other work would be handled inside. Basically his statement is the prevailing paradigm today.

By the 1990s many corporate law departments had developed the capacity to find and manage diverse sources of legal services. Some were handling the majority of the legal needs of their companies, and outside counsel was required mainly for specialized matters which did not justify the maintenance in-house of the necessary expertise, or for time-consuming matters that required more lawyer hours than were available in-house. Major litigation often fell in the latter category. Issues concerning admission to practice in the various states also resulted in use of outside counsel in connection with many litigation matters.

In 2006 the 200 largest corporate law departments in the United States employed 27,700 lawyers. Based on Bureau of Labor Statistics numbers it is estimated that there were approximately 65,000 lawyers employed by businesses in the United States working as lawyers or in other management positions. In 2006, Citigroup had the largest corporate law department in the U.S.A. with 1,500 lawyers, followed by General Electric with 1,200 lawyers and then three insurance companies: Liberty Mutual (775), State Farm (720) and Allstate (700). Exxon was 6th with 600 lawyers.[91] A few in-house law departments are much larger than most Am Law 100 law firms. But the increase in size

---

91 *Analysis of Legal Profession and Law Firms*, HARVARD LAW SCHOOL: PROGRAM ON THE LEGAL PROFESSION (last accessed Dec. 23, 2011), http://www.law.harvard.edu/ programs/plp/pages/statistics.php.

alone does not convey the great increase in importance of corporate law departments. Given the financial and service advantages of bringing legal function in-house, how could it be otherwise?

Today corporate general counsel rule the roost. Some of the leading in-house general counsel earn more than many of the highest paid partners in the major business practice firms, but most do not. Even in cases where the general counsel earns more, there is usually only one attorney at that salary level in their company, whereas the fees paid by client companies to major firms are used to support dozens of equity partners earning leading general counsel level salaries. Stock options and corporate benefits provide additional economic reasons for lawyers to prefer in-house jobs. In addition, working conditions in-house are often superior, and the constant pressure to bring in additional clients and legal work does not exist. Many of my friends from private practice who have gone in-house as general counsel tell me that they much prefer their new roles to the ones they left.

In November of 2011 *The Fulton County Daily Report* published the compensation of 329 general counsel of public companies in eleven Southeastern states (stretching from Virginia to Texas, but omitting Mississippi which did not have any listed general counsel) that filed proxy statements with the Securities and Exchange Commission for 2010. The ten highest paid general counsel in the Southeast had compensation packages averaging approximately $4.9 million with the highest paid receiving $9.2 million and the tenth $3.7 million. There were 16 whose compensation exceeded $3 million, an additional 34 whose compensation exceeded $2 million, and 90 more who received compensation packages of a $1 million or more. Not included were the general counsel of private companies or general counsel of public companies who were not among the five most highly compensated officers of their respective companies.[92]

---

92 Katheryn Hayes Tucker, *The South's Richest General Counsel*, FULTON CNTY. DAILY REP., Nov. 21, 2011, *available at* http://www.law.com/jsp/cc/PubArticleCC. jsp?id=1202532907861.

As corporate counsel jobs have grown more numerous and the quality of the lawyers holding these jobs has increased, the status of in-house lawyers has increased, not only within their companies, but also in their home communities and nationally. The status gap between inside and outside lawyers has largely been reversed. Serving as general counsel of a major business is a more coveted position than serving as a senior partner of most major firms. Some general counsel have stepped into the positions of community leadership formerly held by the partners of major business practice firms.

While many in-house lawyers prefer their working conditions to practicing with a private firm, no one should make the mistake of assuming that the in-house lawyer's life is a picnic. They do not have to spend time on marketing, although good relationships with their colleagues within and without the law department are important to the in-house lawyer's success. In-house law departments outsource to their companies' human resources, finance and other departments many of the administrative responsibilities carried by private practice partners. Nonetheless, one of the senior lawyers in the law department must manage these relationships to obtain sufficient support from other departments. Because of this in-house support, corporate counsel can spend more of their working day on legal work for their client-employer, and still possibly end up working fewer hours, but great pressures and stress can and do exist in-house as well.

WHY AND WHEN TO USE OUTSIDE COUNSEL?

There are several reasons why corporate law departments seek the help of outside counsel. Expertise and capacity are often an issue. As a general rule, if a company has enough of a particular kind of work to keep a lawyer busy full time, its law department will hire a lawyer to do the work in-house if it can find one with the necessary experience and skills at an acceptable price. If a company has a sudden substantial but temporary project it is likely to hire an outside firm rather than significantly overload its law department staff or make a hurried hiring decision.

If a company has a "bet-the-company" issue, corporate general counsel may seek the most experienced and successful firm dealing with such matters to maximize the prospects of obtaining the best possible result. In the past such a project might have been turned over to outside counsel in its entirety. Today corporate counsel is more likely to divide the work to be done between inside and outside lawyers based on availability and capability and to expect the collaborative support of outside counsel.

One of my colleagues, John Hopkins, previously served as general counsel for one of the largest shareholder-owned insurance companies in the United States. He tells me that in his role as general counsel he divided his company's hundred or so pending defense cases into two categories—routine life insurance or ERISA claims that didn't pose any major threat (commodity work in his view) and consumer class actions that, if mishandled, posed real financial peril. For the former he instructed his in-house litigation supervisors to seek out the lowest cost but experienced insurance defense counsel in the community (typically a partner in a very small insurance defense firm with low rates). For the latter matters he sought the most experienced and talented large-case, class-action litigator from any U.S. jurisdiction and created a "virtual law firm" by combining the resources of his law department, of a highly regarded local litigator, and of the lawyer that he thought had the highest degree of relevant insurance consumer class action expertise.

I believed, as a GC, that it was my duty to *my client* to procure the highest quality legal service for the most reasonable price. But you have to seek a reasonable balance. Routine commodity work doesn't justify a highest-quality at all costs approach, and truly important matters do—so costs are a less relevant consideration in important matters.[93]

John's comments illustrate two important themes. First, that general counsel are cost-driven when that makes sense and cannot be loyal to a regular outside major law firm whose cost structure would make them non-competitive for commodity work. And second, the general counsel also gives no thought to his company's major outside law firm in a bet-the-company case, either for the lead local litigator or for the peculiar subject matter expertise, if it is not the best firm for the work to be done. I believe the fact that in the bet-the-company case cost was not an influencing factor explains why some highly-expert smaller firms can be quite successful financially without significant leverage. And it further illustrates that, while convenience and human relationships may be factors, most corporate general counsel attempt to select the most competent lawyers for the job at hand at the best price regardless of firm size.

Kent Alexander, then a Senior Vice President and General Counsel of Emory University, described his law department's process this way in 2008:

---

93 John D. Hopkins served as General Counsel to the Jefferson Pilot Corporation from 1993-2003. He is a graduate of the University of Virginia Law School and is a partner in Taylor English Duma LLP. He was a partner in King & Spalding in Atlanta and in Washington, D.C. and co-head of the firm's corporate practice for many years. He has also been prominent nationally in continuing legal education in the corporate arena.

We have done many of the things I think most corporate counsel do: in-source more work, create more contract templates for internal clients, hold beauty contests among outside counsel (cost and quality can vary dramatically), counter-intuitively insist on more effort from the more senior partners (to save the hours), cap fees up front, share in risk/reward when filing suits, rely on outside counsel for arm chair roles (as opposed to full engagement roles), renegotiate bills when they appear bloated and look to solo or small firm practitioners, not just large firms.[94]

For those companies without an in-house lawyer, dealing with a firm large enough to serve all of the client's needs may be something of a blessing. However, most clients utilizing Am Law 200 firms have their own law departments. For these larger clients the advantages of employing large outside firms are limited.

In selecting outside counsel, the issues are usually competence, capacity, cost, and service. Competence is the bedrock issue. But how is competence defined today? Competence is not merely experience and knowledge; it is a combination of subject-area expertise, sound analysis and good judgment, strong case/project management skills and the communication and social skills necessary to relate well to the client.

Changing lawyers or law firms is inconvenient, disruptive and time consuming for corporate counsel. Doing so infringes on the time required to do their job of addressing legal issues, is often unpleasant, and making a change does not guarantee that the

---

94 Katheryn Hayes Tucker, *Standardized Work, Cost Cutting Alter GC Relationship With Outside Counsel*, FULTON CNTY. DAILY REP., Oct. 27, 2008.

problems experienced with existing outside counsel will not continue or grow worse with a new one.

There are advantages to continuing to work with lawyers whose capabilities, judgment and ethics are known to you. You know from experience which lawyers in your former firm you can trust to do a good job at a reasonable cost and those you cannot. This type of knowledge can be obtained with respect to a new outside firm only from experience. It is easier and quicker to retain existing counsel. Bill Jacobs, the retired General Counsel of EMS Technologies, Inc. told me that: "I think you are right about the importance in sticking with an outside counsel because of such factors as familiarity, personal loyalties, and the uncertainties and time involved in shopping around."[95] If the relationship isn't broken, don't try to fix it.

Phil Moise, the General Counsel of Immucor, Inc., who has focused on the process of selecting outside counsel, described his process this way:

> High on my list is manageability; that is, whether I can manage the relationship to get the desired services at the desired costs .... [T]his is also important to other corporate counsel because it's all about managing the cost. What leads to better manageability? Knowing the law firm or the lead lawyer for a long time; knowing the market; talking to other general counsels; having a personality that allows you to talk bluntly to outside lawyers who want to do it their way, etc. When I

---

95 E-mail from William S. Jacobs to author (Dec. 31, 2010) (on file with author). William S. Jacobs served for 14 years as General Counsel of EMS Technologies, Inc. He is a graduate of the Duke Law School who clerked for Judge Griffin Bell, United States Court of Appeals for the Fifth Circuit, and then for Associate Justice William H. Rehnquist of the United States Supreme Court. He was a partner in the law firm of Trotter Smith & Jacobs before becoming the General Counsel of EMS Technologies.

moved in-house and continued to use my former firm for most of our work, the CEO thought I was just trying to help my old friends. I had to explain that my long-term relationship with the lawyers at my former firm allowed me to know who to use and who not to use, and how to best manage the billing since I knew their margins and how far they were likely to go in discounting fees.[96]

Once sufficient competence (including manageability) has been established, cost is the most important consideration.

Many corporate law departments prefer not to concentrate the work of their company in one or a few outside firms. This change is attributable to several factors including cost, service and judgment considerations; the diverse employment backgrounds of the in-house lawyers; the desire to hire the best talent available at the best price; and the personal preferences and friendships of the in-house lawyers doing the hiring. On those occasions when corporate counsel need outside help for commodity work, they usually look for reliable low cost firms. For more specialized work they look for firms with a high level of expertise and a record of success in the relevant legal field.

It is very unusual today for a single outside firm to do all or even most of the work farmed out by a major client to outside counsel. Only on the most important legal matters affecting a client will senior outside counsel have direct contact with senior executives of a major company. The effect of this change in relationships is to relegate outside counsel to a specialist role advising in-house lawyers and to

96 E-mail from Philip H. Moise, Exec. Vice President, Gen. Counsel & Sec'y, Immucor, Inc., to author (June 28, 2011) (on file with author). Philip H. Moise is a Duke Law School graduate who was a partner in Trotter Smith & Jacobs; Long & Aldridge; and Nelson Mullins before becoming a partner in Sutherland.

reduce or eliminate the role of most senior management (other than the general counsel and his or her staff) in the selection, management and compensation of outside counsel.

Soaring costs have also encouraged corporate law departments as well as outside counsel to substitute contract and subcontracted lawyers provided by placement agencies for more expensive corporate counsel or lawyer-employees. Contract lawyers now handle significant work under the supervision of inside corporate counsel or outside counsel, and law departments and private practice firms now use document systems and non-lawyer personnel including paralegals and document clerks to provide legal services to their clients. In 2010 forty-four percent of the firms responding to the Altman Weil Flash Survey reported use of contract lawyers and 28 percent added part-time lawyers. Fifty-nine percent stated an intention to use contract lawyers in 2011.[97] The outsourcing of legal services by law firms is also increasing, often to Indian lawyers, but increasingly in the United States as well.

Some corporate law departments are experimenting with programs to reduce the number of outside firms they employ in expectation of improved services and a lower overall cost from the favored firms. Such convergence programs are currently popular in the corporate counsel world, but they are not a panacea. Most corporate general counsel moved their departments away from exclusive relationships with one or a few firms in order to gain control over the legal services provided to their company by reducing the influence of the outside firms. However, after clearly establishing their control of their employer's legal work the general counsels of DuPont, General Electric, Cisco and Pfizer, among others, have moved back toward the use of fewer outside firms.

---

97 Thomas Clay & Eric A. Seeger, *2011 Law Firms in Transition: An Altman Weil Flash Survey*, ALTMAN WEIL, INC., at 5-6..

It is rare today for a partner from a major firm to serve on the board of directors of a company represented by his or her firm. This is another sign of the growing prominence of corporate counsel. After years of persistent wrestling with the private practice bar over corporate counsels' ability and prerogative to manage the legal affairs of their companies, corporate counsel in most companies have prevailed. Most of them have demonstrated their competence and resolve to do their job well and their ability to manage the legal affairs of their companies. In the 1970s and 1980s, during the transition to in-house leadership in legal matters, many skirmishes of this sort took place. Most have now been put to rest.

On the whole this is bad news for outside counsel. They are being told how they can staff the projects in which they are involved and with whom. Their control over pricing has been diminished. While some of the leading spokespersons on the corporate side are sincerely talking about building better and more constructive relationships with outside counsel, most expect these better relationships to yield lower costs. It is hard to see how costs can be reduced without reducing the profitability of the outside firms.

In addition, disaggregation and collaboration between inside and outside counsel is becoming an important approach to reducing the total cost of legal projects and the involvement of outside counsel. Corporate counsel increasingly expect to handle those aspects of a legal project that they can do cost-effectively. They expect outside counsel to provide support where needed rather than having outside counsel assume responsibility for the entire project. Depending on the situation corporate counsel may do all of the document review, legal research and electronic discovery relating to a litigation matter (or outsource it to a low cost service provider) while looking to outside counsel for experience with the presentation of such cases. Corporate counsel may also divide among several firms the work to be done by private firms on the same project.

Where the client and its law department want to distance themselves from the resolution of a dispute or negotiation, outside counsel may participate or actually handle negotiation or trial. In corporate transactional work corporate counsel might handle the due diligence, legal research, and the initial drafting of documents. Outside counsel might be asked to assist with drafting specific terms and to provide advice and negotiation assistance. Achieving an appropriate balance in such collaboration requires corporate counsel able to manage such relationships and outside counsel willing to be managed.

The era has ended when major firms could expect to provide all of the legal services required to accomplish a transaction or resolve a dispute while enjoying the profits on the commodity work relating to the project. The commodity portions are likely to be farmed out to more cost-effective service providers or retained in-house.

RESETTING THE RELATIONSHIP BETWEEN CORPORATE COUNSEL AND OUTSIDE COUNSEL

Among the current organized efforts to reset the relationship between corporate law departments and outside counsel covered by the legal press are the Association of Corporate Counsel's "Value Challenge" and the model created by the Pfizer Legal Alliance. The purpose of the ACC Value Challenge is to restructure the law firm-client relationship. As Susan Hackett, General Counsel of the Association stated in an interview published in the December 2008 edition of *The American Lawyer*:

Take a look at the cost of legal services and the fact they they've been rising 6, 7, 8 percent a year, for as long as anyone can remember. But the services remain pretty much the same. And at the same time that outside firms' costs are rising, the in-house law departments are getting better at their efficiencies and at lowering their costs. But they don't see the law firms with any motivation to increase their efficiency.[98]

Hackett states that the ACC's law firm profitability model was designed to show that:

you can improve efficiency and therefore save clients money by charging lower fees, and at the same time you can make the firm more profitable. How could that not be a win-win for everyone?

What the model shows . . . is that the larger law firms that are operating with quite a large number of associates – most of whom won't make partner – have a very high attrition rate. They pay out huge expenses to attract and hire and train associates. So if that associate leaves before spending four or five years with the firm, the firm loses money on them. And guess who's paying for that? Clients who didn't want them on their work in the first place. It's a crazy situation.

The model suggests that you remove some of that attrition by hiring fewer people. Then you can invest more in them to ensure that they stay and can

98   Sue Reisinger, *Peace Talks*, AM. LAW., Dec. 2008, at 102, 102-103.

contribute to profit. You will make enough savings to pass on some to your client, while the profitability of the firm as a whole goes up.

The model also suggests that law firms should "re-equitize" the middle of the firm . . . .

The model shows that if you start to re-equitize the workers in the middle, there may be some slippage at the top level of the partnership, but the vast majority of partners at the firm will make more money.[99]

It sounds so easy, but there are many important compromises in this apparently simple proposal. From the point of view of many of the major business practice firms, the problem is that the "the vast majority" are nonequity partners, counsel and associates, and "the slippage at the top level of the partnership" affects the highly paid equity partners who control the firms' business. A few major firms have been able to operate with great financial success following a model similar to that proposed by the ACC—firms like Wachtell, Munger Tolles, and Williams & Connolly—but can hundreds of other major firms do the same?

Another major reset initiative has been the "Legal Alliance" led by the law department of Pfizer and its general counsel, Amy Schulman. The Pfizer law department is given a fixed annual budget and is expected to manage within its budget regardless of what happens over the course of the year. The stated purpose of the program is lower costs, more collaboration and better value for Pfizer and its outside lawyers. The company's law department has selected 19 firms; each paid an annual flat fee to handle all of the work assigned to it. Pfizer

---

99 *Id.*

took its standard procurement contract and revised it thoroughly to fit its objectives for legal services.

The annual fee that Pfizer pays to each of its selected firms is based on estimates of the type and volume of work that a firm will be responsible for during the year. The firms provide monthly bills so that the amount of their effort and investment can be monitored. If the amount of work they are required to do in their area significantly exceeds what had been expected at the beginning of the year, Pfizer will initiate adjustments based on fairness, but not based on hourly billing rates. The budgets are all-inclusive including disbursements except for expert witness fees in some cases. Any Pfizer corporate counsel can on routine matters consult with any attorney of a participating Alliance law firm without an adjustment in the compensation the Alliance firm. The Pfizer law department holds back approximately 20% of its budgeted spend to allow for bonuses, adjustments in the anticipated volume of work and to reward commitment to and cooperation in the joint effort.[100]

The Pfizer Alliance actually encourages cross-selling. Pfizer sponsors regular events for Alliance members, Pfizer corporate counsel, and Pfizer's outside firms. Many of the firms offer additional services on a trial basis at no charge which gives Pfizer's law department the opportunity to work with new lawyers and judge their competence and manageability. If Pfizer is happy with the work performed, it is factored into the firm's bonus for the year and into the flat fee for the following year.

In many respects the Pfizer Legal Alliance is a throwback to the retainer relationships that existed in the 1950s and 1960s between major clients and their principal outside law firms. The firms provided most of the services required by their clients for fixed annual payments that were examined and reset annually.

---

100 Amy Miller, *No More Baby Sitters*, AM. LAW., Dec. 2009, at 66, 66-70.

Both of these initiatives reflect dissatisfaction of corpoᵣate counsel and their employers with the cost of legal services provided by private practice firms. They are designed first and foremost to retain major business practice firms that will cooperate with their clients in reducing the costs of such services while maintaining or improving the quality of the service. These arrangements have the added advantage of encouraging outside counsel to be efficient in the provision of their services.

Clients using expert services want access to seasoned lawyers and do not want to pay for the work of inexperienced young attorneys at the levels they now pay, if at all. Consequently, the mix of lawyers will change. There will be more corporate counsel. As for private practice lawyers and their firms, there will be fewer of them providing legal services to mature businesses, a lower percentage of associates, a higher percentage of partners, and lower compensation for most of those who remain. Through this transition, there will also be many law school graduates who will not be employed as lawyers.

For a variety of reasons outlined in Chapter Four, making such changes is easier said than done. Unwinding the generations of legacy policies and costs built into the New York Model is very difficult. Despite the financial bonanza enjoyed by many major business practice firms over the past ten years, I believe there is likely to be a steady downward trend in the average Profits Per Partner of the majority of these firms. Many will not survive. This will occur because of the excess supply of talented lawyers, the growing sophistication of major purchasers of legal services, and other factors discussed in this book.

CHAPTER ELEVEN

Commoditization

The commoditization of legal services is one of the most important developments exerting influence on the legal profession and on the profitability of major business practice law firms. As companies have grown larger and more complex there are increasing incentives to develop standardized solutions to recurring legal issues and transactions.

Corporate counsel are motivated to develop standardized solutions for use by their companies. To the extent that corporate counsel utilize the services of private practice attorneys, finding outside lawyers who can provide very good work at a reasonable price is a major objective. Firms that have already developed such solutions and can make them available to new clients with a minimum of customizing are going to be hired before lawyers who treat each document for each new client as an individualized work of art. The advantage to the client of lawyers who have standardized products capable of rapid customization is akin to semiconductor manufacturers that make programmable logic devices.

For more than a century, a process has been underway in U.S. law that has led to the commoditization of many legal services. There are several pieces to this continuing and accelerating process. I define "legal commodities" as legal services that have become so standardized in concept and execution that any one of a number of law firms can produce a good enough version to meet the needs of most clients. As a result law firms are increasingly being forced to compete on price for the opportunity to do such work. The effect is that the economic value realized by lawyers providing these services has and will continue to decline and the shelf-life and economic value of many services that are highly specialized today will dwindle as they are in turn standardized, and then commoditized.

The precursor of commoditization is standardization. Standardization occurs when the forms and procedures that serve to document a particular type of transaction have become uniform and have been used repeatedly over a significant period of time. Commoditization does not occur from further improvements in such forms and procedures, but rather from the changing point of view of the consumers of such services. When a client concludes that there are at least several qualified suppliers of the service, and the only significant selection considerations are price and date of delivery, the service has become a commodity.

Of course there is always the possibility that something unanticipated could occur, but it is not necessary that a standardized document or procedure be foolproof in order for it to become a legal commodity. And even within a largely commoditized document or transaction, there may be an issue that requires the services of a true expert. Corporate counsel are increasingly sensitive to the disaggregation of such issues from the transaction in which they arise. The existence of a single important and complex issue in a document or transaction does not require that the entire document or transaction must be handled by a firm that specializes in that issue. Collaboration between corporate counsel and an expert firm is often the best solution.

The groundwork for standardization in the United States began with efforts in the late 1800s to harmonize the laws of the various states by the adoption of uniform state laws and by subsequent efforts to clarify and simplify the laws in most frequent use. The American Bar Association began in 1889 to work for "uniformity of the laws" as it promoted the Conference of State Boards of Commissioners for Promoting Uniformity of Law. This effort was strengthened by the creation of the American Law Institute in 1923. The Institute's express purpose was "to promote the clarification and simplification of the law and its better adaptation to social needs . . . ."[101]

However, midway through the 20th century efforts to clarify and simplify the law were being made by a legal profession that was still composed of a multitude of firms that would be considered small by today's standards. At that time most businesses did not need to consult a lawyer every week, or even every month and litigation had not become a pervasive part of doing business. While a number of the major business practice firms in New York City offered services beyond their own region, most local and regional businesses used law firms based in their city or region. Regional differences existed with respect to the law and how it was practiced.

Today every Am Law 100 firm and many smaller firms seek business wherever they can find it in the United States and abroad. As the practices of many firms have evolved from local or regional to national and international, many local and regional differences

---

101 *About the American Law Institute*, AM. L. INST., http://www.ali.org/ali/thisali. htm (last visited Jan. 15, 2012).

have disappeared and national and international standards and expectations have evolved. In many industries a small group of law firms have become the recognized leaders; the solutions, documents and procedures they have developed for their clients (which have been readily available to their competitors) have become the national and international standards for such industries. While lawyers might want to create unique documents to deal with their clients' transactions, clients frequently reach the conclusion that the tweaks are not worth the expense. The more standardized the solutions have become, the greater the possibility of legal documents and procedures becoming commodities.

In the process, practitioners of law moved from being an array of very small partnerships providing customized and individualized legal services into a major industry of multi-million (even billion) dollar institutions subject to many of the same economic forces and influences that have shaped other service providers in our consumer economy.

Another factor that has contributed to the standardization of many legal services in the United States has been the huge increase in both the number of lawyers in the United States and in the number of lawyers relative to the population. As a result of the growth in the number of lawyers, law schools, and legal publications, most legal issues receive much more intense and immediate attention today than they could have received 60 years ago, and this has contributed to the standardization and commoditization of maturing areas of practice.

In the 21st century all substantial businesses require daily legal advice and planning and a frequent and steady response to, or use of, litigation. Because of litigation's important role in managing business relationships and competition, many large businesses have hundreds of lawsuits pending at any given time. Modern law departments were created by businesses to deal cost-effectively with the increased volume and complexity of the many legal issues they face.

THE ROLE OF CORPORATE COUNSEL IN THE STANDARDIZATION OF U.S. LAW

As already noted, higher costs and the desire to obtain better control over their legal issues caused businesses to bring much of their legal function in-house. A few very large companies had corporate counsel prior to World War II, primarily to select and oversee the work of outside counsel. Following the war there was a slow but steady increase in the utilization of corporate counsel and corporate law departments.

Over time major businesses have replaced their outside general counsel with corporate counsel who have become their companies' principal legal advisors. Corporate management looks to corporate counsel to harmonize legal issues with the company's business operations and to control and reduce legal costs. In addition, corporate counsel have become the arbiters of their companies' relationships with outside counsel. They are more knowledgeable, astute and discerning purchasers of legal services than the legally unschooled corporate executives who previously purchased outside legal services.

The need to deal with soaring legal expenses has trumped the traditional way companies have acquired and utilized legal services, and has reduced the tolerance of corporate counsel for individualized legal work except for the most important matters. "Very good" solutions are often "good enough." However, pressures on outside counsel to reduce the time spent on legal projects in order to be "efficient" have raised the risk of error and of potential malpractice liability.[102] At some point, corporate law departments may find themselves caught up in the responsibility for errors that may be caused by their insistence on "efficient" representation, but for now the outside firms and their insurers are bearing most of such risk.

Not only can complex and individualized legal products be expensive to create, but they are also often difficult and expensive to manage and support over time. It is clear that the complex and immature documents and concepts used to create and administer collateralized debt obligations and credit default swaps contributed significantly to the financial debacle of recent years. If a legal product requires one of the country's leading legal specialists to understand it, the product is far too complicated to use in most commercial transactions. Imagine how some trial court judges or juries might struggle with a dispute involving complex derivatives. How would they understand and interpret the documentation and reach an appropriate result? Consequently, thoughtful corporate counsel are not only looking for legal products that are "good enough:" they are also looking for products that are "simple enough" to be understood and used by their company's employees and customers.

In his 2007 speech at a Northwestern University School of Law conference, Cisco's General Counsel, Mark Chandler, emphasized these points when he stated that:

> First, winners [among law firms] will be those who are able to standardize services to meet clients' cost management and predictability needs where very good is good enough . . . . All around the periphery of the legal industry, standardization of information

---

102 See, e.g., Kristi E. Swartz, Lawsuit: Thrashers Owners Have Been Trying to Sell Team Since 2005, Jan. 22, 2011, http://www.ajc.com/sports/lawsuit-thrashers-owners-have-811606.html (discussing $200 million malpractice lawsuit against King and Spalding).

is happening .... Our goal will be accomplished by standardization of forms and open interfaces, making a smooth multi-vendor operation out of what had been a series of job shops.[103]

And the more this happens the easier it is for corporate law departments to perform the work themselves.

As some corporate counsel have come to think of their business with outside counsel more as the purchase of a product than the receipt of services, more clients are requesting bids for the product from several qualified firms. In some cases procurement departments of the businesses seeking legal services now run the actual selection process.

Those firms that have found ways to produce very good services for less cost have become more attractive to corporate counsel, creating pressure on other outside counsel to find ways to reduce the cost of their services as well. As law firms find it increasingly necessary to compete on price, they are driven to find standardized solutions to their clients' legal needs at prices consistent with their clients' expectations and their own requirements.

The growing use of document systems and of non-legal personnel to manage transactions has contributed to the capacity on one hand, and the necessity on the other, to standardize and commoditize many legal services. Indeed, such standardization and most commoditization could not have taken place without the technological improvements applied to the practice of law in recent times.

Because businesses must constantly seek to reduce costs, corporate counsel have a strong motivation to find ways to standardize legal

---

103 Mark Chandler, Gen. Counsel of Cisco Sys., Inc., Address at the Northwestern School of Law Securities Regulation Institute: State of Technology in Law (Jan. 25, 2007), *available at* http://blogs.cisco.com/news/cisco_general_counsel_on_state_of_technology_in_the_law/.

services, whether the services are created inside or purchased from outside firms. This motivation is the most powerful contributor to the growing standardization and resulting commoditization of U.S. law.

EXPANSION OF RESOURCES AVAILABLE TO LAWYERS TO IMPROVE THEIR SKILLS AND THE QUALITY OF THEIR SERVICES

The explosion in the quantity and quality of legal literature and of continuing legal education opportunities and resources over the past 50 years has expanded and strengthened the foundations upon which the standardization of U.S. law has been built. Prior to World War II, the sources of legal knowledge were relatively few (statutes, judicial decisions, law school case books, law reviews, and a few loose leaf services and treatises on some subjects). As a result, less of the law was documented and available, and more of it was in the memories of the much smaller number of lawyers then in practice.

A. Publications. Today most corporate counsel and major firms have access to large amounts of legal information such as the databases provided by LexisNexis and WestLaw. They also have powerful software tools for searching and organizing the materials available to them. As a result, lawyers have quick and easy access to a vastly increased supply of useful and reliable legal resources including catalogs of forms and publications providing extensive guidance about managing transactions.

In the late 1920s there were approximately 80 legal periodicals in print. Today there are so many that there is a loose-leaf service devoted solely to identifying the loose-leaf services available – *Legal Looseleafs in Print* published by Infosources Publishing. This service tells us that there are over 3,600 loose-leaf legal publications from 270 different publishers. In addition there are nearly 1,000 law reviews/ journals in publication and more than 2,200 legal newsletters, plus some 1,400 monographs published each year. The Westlaw service can provide access to 16,700 legal, financial and business news databases, while LexisNexis can provide customers access to over five billion searchable documents from more than 32,000 legal, news and business sources.

In addition to these greatly enhanced traditional sources of legal information, we now also have thousands of blogs addressing legal issues. The cover story in the December 2010 edition of the *American Bar Association Journal* was the 4th Annual *Blawg 100*[104] and it reports that there were more than 3,000 legal blogs being published in the United States.

With every lawyer and every firm able to consult and rely upon the same pool of resources, the universal availability of these materials encourages standardization. Moreover, the imposing number of sources available compels lawyers to simplify their approaches to the practice whenever and however they can.

B. The Effects of Continuing Legal Education and Law Firm Marketing Programs. Prior to 1933 there were few continuing legal education programs or publications. As a result, most training was on the job. There were as many solutions to legal problems as there were law firms to address them.

The Practicing Law Institute was chartered by the Regents of the State University of New York in 1933 and began its programs and publications shortly thereafter. The volume and variety of these programs and publications has expanded dramatically since its founding.

---

104 Molly McDonough & Sarah Randag, *The Blawg 100*, ABA JOURNAL, Dec. 2010, at 33, 33-39.

Beginning in 1947 the American Law Institute and the American Bar Association have cooperated in offering a national program of continuing legal education. They created a joint American Law Institute-American Bar Association Committee on Continuing Professional Education that produces books, periodicals, and audiovisual materials relating to most areas of the law, and offers courses of study and program of instruction throughout the country. The ABA itself also operates a large press producing hundreds of legal publications annually.

Most state bar associations hopped on the CLE bandwagon. In 1965 the Georgia Bar created the Institute for Continuing Legal Education in Georgia. Dozens of programs approved for CLE credit by the State Bar of Georgia are presented annually to Georgia lawyers. Many state bar associations operate similar programs. There is also a variety of for-profit companies that provide legal training programs that are available to the profession. Many industry associations sponsor forums for the discussion of their legal issues, and they have found that their members and their lawyers (inside or out) welcome opportunities to participate and showcase their knowledge.

Consequently, the profession has benefited from a great increase in the number and type of continuing legal education programs that have played an important role in bringing lawyers together from all over the country to study and explore solutions to legal issues. The forms and materials distributed in conjunction with these programs have been used by lawyers all over the United States in their practices. These gatherings have encouraged the creation of uniform legal documents, processes and procedures across the United States— further facilitating the standardization of U.S. law.

There is another equally important way in which continuing legal education has contributed to the standardization of legal services in the United States. Prior to the 1970s when the canons of ethics of many state bar associations prohibited lawyers from soliciting (directly or indirectly) the business of non-clients, lawyers realized that one of the most effective ways of circumventing these restrictions was to appear on continuing legal education panels and on industry educational programs, and to write articles on legal issues for law reviews, legal journals and industry publications. When the canons were changed in the 1970s to permit direct solicitation, and as in-house staffs grew in number and size, this practice grew in strength and volume. Every firm encourages its lawyers to participate in these programs, and many firms have sponsored and produced their own conferences for corporate counsel and business executives.

However, by participating in these programs the law firms have armed competitor law firms with much of the knowledge and know-how such firms need to compete more effectively, and they also have armed the private practice firms' most significant competitors—in-house law departments—with much of the knowledge and know-how they might otherwise have had to purchase from private practice firms. It is common practice for individual lawyers and firms to use the materials supplied to them by these programs to address the needs of their own clients. In the process good forms (and some not so good) are used again and again and become standards for the practice. One of my colleagues who helped real estate investment trusts with their securities offerings likes to tell of reviewing prior filings to prepare himself for a new offering and finding many, obviously copied, that contained the same typographical errors.

As a result of the outstanding system of continuing legal education in the United States and our greatly expanded access to authoritative legal reference materials, any lawyer and any law firm in the United States with reasonable intelligence and energy can quickly become an expert on most legal matters. This phenomenon has shortened the shelf life of most legal specialties and has hastened the transformation of many of them into standardized and commoditized products and services.

C. Document and Knowledge Management. Also of great importance today are the document and knowledge management systems of corporate law departments and law firms. Lawyers in organizations with highly developed systems are able to save into central, networked drives copies of important memorandums of law, agreements, pleadings, or other documents created by or provided to the department or firm. If carefully classified and indexed, these documents can easily be identified and retrieved by any lawyer or legal assistant working for their organization. Many firms identify which of the forms preserved in the document management system are appropriate for use in particular circumstances. The best systems contain standardized and annotated documents with instructions concerning alternative provisions and their uses in particular situations. Clients are now sponsoring information networks that are shared by the client and all of its outside law firms handling particular projects or types of work. The use of these knowledge management tools has encouraged the standardization of many types of documents.

D. Commercial Knowledge Management Services. New online knowledge management services are resulting in extraordinary improvements in the availability of information and knowledge about transactions and legal issues. These services are creating greatly improved methods of conveying best practices to lawyers around the world and speeding the acceptance and use of such practices. The services are comprehensive in their coverage, they are maintained effectively on a real-time basis, and they can be tailored to incorporate the unique knowledge and experience of each participating firm.

Only a few years ago, a lawyer faced with a problem could seek guidance first among his professional colleagues, then in his library of available publications, and could attend a CLE program sponsored by his State Bar Association or the Practicing Law Institute (among others sources), or peruse his firm's files of collected materials or its online database. Today commercial programs make it possible to do all of these things plus others on one site in real time while sitting at one's desk.

For instance, the *Practical Law Company* subscription service provides a full corporate document and issue service maintained by a large group of lawyers employed by the company and augmented by a panel of distinguished practitioners who are partners in some of the best known corporate firms in the United States. A lawyer who subscribes to this or similar services can research online a type of transaction, a document he needs to prepare, or a legal issue and immediately get much of the information, examples and practical advice he requires. Unlike publications, these services are updated to provide the latest available information, and the insights of experts, in hours instead of weeks or months.

Until recently the very best of the major business practice firms created and maintained internal knowledge management programs for the exclusive use of their own lawyers and clients. It is difficult and very expensive to maintain these programs for the limited use of one firm. Firms having such capabilities found themselves in increasing demand by corporate counsel requiring the most up-to-date information and knowledge about particular legal issues or transactions. Now, for a relatively modest annual fee, these integrated services are available for the asking to any lawyer, any law firm or any law department in the English-speaking world.

The effect cannot be overstated. The good news is that every lawyer can now have at his or her disposal most of the knowledge and experience that previously was available only to the few firms with the clientele and financial resources required to compile and maintain significant private resources for their own limited use. Now firms, rather than attempting (and often failing) to create their own treasure trove of knowledge and experience, can access a vastly greater resource for only a fraction of the cost and effort previously required. Many will use a commercially available program as their basic resource and supplement it with refinements of their own. There will still be intense competition on the margins for very specialized knowledge, but the playing field has been leveled. It is inevitable that every major practice area will be served by one or more of these services.

The bad news is that the playing field has been leveled. The existence of these capabilities supplied by subscription services should greatly increase competition among legal service providers and further strengthen the drive toward commoditization. Corporate counsel also have access to these same services and use them, reducing their need for access to private practice expertise. The consequence will be a significant reduction in the need for private practice services for companies with their own law departments.

The considerable complexity, commitment and costs of building rival knowledge management programs have been a major differentiator between the most successful firms and their competitors. Access to such collections of knowledge and experience has been a primary reason for corporate counsel to establish and maintain relationships with major business practice firms. The game has now been fundamentally changed.

The tremendous growth in the availability and usability of legal knowledge has affected and will continue to affect the way legal services are provided in the United States. Fifty years ago it might have taken a lawyer or firm years, if not decades, to achieve the same level of awareness and knowledge about particular legal issues and transactions that can be obtained in a few hours today. Our well-educated bar is drawn to the best solutions and is able to find them quickly. Consequently, it is not surprising that many legal services are becoming standardized products and then commodities.

THE EFFECTS OF HIGH LEVERAGE AND HIGH ATTRITION

A strategic operating decision made by almost every major business practice law firm in the U.S. has contributed greatly to the standardization and commoditization of legal services in the United States. Most have adopted the New York Model that relies heavily on associate leverage. They utilize associates to provide a high percentage of their services, and they restrict the growth of their partnerships in order to increase their Profits Per Partner (and in the process encourage most of their associates after a few years sojourn to seek other employment).

As a result, the number of partners available to review and edit associate work has declined relative to the number of associates, causing standardization to become an increasingly important and necessary tool of law firm management, replacing direct partner review and oversight. The supervision and training that most young associates receive is from other associates with four to eight years of experience. Document and knowledge management systems have enabled both in-house and outside legal counsel to move work downstream to less experienced lawyers who are not authorized to modify the forms they have been instructed to use without the consent of a partner or a more senior associate. The widespread use of legal assistants and other non-lawyer personnel to prepare legal documents and manage aspects of legal projects has further increased the need for greater standardization of documents, processes and procedures.

Consequently, private practice firms themselves have come to rely on standardization in the management of their practices.

The policy of high leverage and high attrition has further contributed to standardization by flooding the legal job market with thousands of able-enough young lawyers with significant-enough experience with major legal transactions to compete with their former employers either as corporate counsel or at other law firms. Rather than locking these folks up and throwing away the key, the major firms have enthusiastically pushed them out the door into the arms of their competitors. This dispersal of talented and knowledgeable lawyers quickly spreads the latest knowledge and know-how about every type of legal issue and transaction. These lawyers naturally tend to continue doing documents and transactions the way they experienced them with their original firms, especially those who have worked for the more prominent firms in their respective fields. Consequently, high leverage and high attrition have greatly increased the number of law firms and legal departments that are capable of handling specific types of transactions in the standard manner.

TECHNOLOGY

Technology has removed many of the remaining barriers to the standardization of legal services. High costs have been the driving force behind standardization, but technology has greatly facilitated it. The most important recent technology developments have been the Internet and e-mail which have made it possible for lawyers (inside and outside) to quickly find the latest knowledge about most legal matters and the latest versions of related documents, and to share them within their organizations and with their clients quickly.

The drive toward standardization and commoditization is restrained by the increasing complexity of the business, financial and regulatory worlds. New challenges, new ideas, new solutions, and new documents appear regularly. As older problems are resolved, standardized and commoditized new fads or fancies appear that require thoughtful analysis, new solutions and new structures. These processes take time. A simple problem and its solution may be standardized in a year or two, and become a commodity soon thereafter. But the many continuing problems with collateralized mortgages, other securitized debt obligations, and credit default swaps tell us that the process of standardization and commoditization for some transactions may take years instead of months. As has been true with derivatives, the market sometimes proceeds as though the legal product had been commoditized when in fact the inherent issues, complications and processes have not been sorted out sufficiently for the product to be used so quickly and so thoughtlessly in so many financially significant transactions.

Howard Darmstadter's comments in his excellent article in the November 2010 edition of *The Business Lawyer* could not be more apropos to this issue:

> The heyday of securitization has passed, or at least been interrupted. But for a time, where there was a payment obligation, it seemed that there was also an investment banker bent on packaging and securitizing it. Increasingly complex structures were devised to tailor the product more closely to the needs of particular investor while conforming to complex regulatory and tax requirements.
>
> These complex structures called forth complex documents ....

> How well did legal drafters meet these challenges? In particular, were the documents easily comprehensible? Unambiguous? Arithmetically accurate?
>
> This isn't a mystery novel, so I'll give you the answers right now. The documents were almost comically incomprehensible, frequently ambiguous, and occasionally produced the wrong numbers.
>
> The first answer should surprise no one. Given the complexity of the structures, the documents were always going to be hard to read. But an impossible read? It is not clear that anyone, including their drafters, fully understood those documents.[105]

For hundreds of years, lawyers have been the indispensable intermediaries between the knowledge necessary to successfully navigate the legal system and the entities and individuals in need of that knowledge. Lawyers have also been the experts applying such knowledge to real world situations. Some lawyers have had better and more complete access to such knowledge than others. This is one reason why we have thought of legal work as a professional service rather than a product.

As the developments outlined in this chapter have taken root and interacted with one another, the fundamental dynamics of the legal profession have been permanently altered. These developments are making it possible for more lawyers, including in-house lawyers, to acquire and apply the accumulated knowledge of the legal system

---

105 Howard Darmstadter, *Precision's Counterfeit: The Failure of Complex Documents, and Some Suggested Remedies*, 66 Bus. Law. 61, 61-62 (Nov. 2010).

much more rapidly and knowledgeably at a lower cost. They will also enable clients to do more of their own work, and for alternative non-professional service providers to encroach on the private practice firm domain. For example, Legal Zoom, founded around 2006, has helped over one million customers with incorporation, wills and living trusts, intellectual property filings and other standardized legal documents.

The confluence of these developments has enabled clients to fundamentally restructure the way in which they purchase, receive and use legal services, and to better control the costs of acquiring them. This process has led to the standardization of most legal services and to the commoditization of many of them, and this process will surely continue. There will always be a limited number of legal issues and opportunities that will command the services of very highly qualified and highly specialized private practice attorneys. Successful litigators will always be in demand. These lawyers will populate the top quality boutiques envisioned by Mark Chandler at Cisco.

Under these circumstances, how much specialized work will be needed from outside counsel and how many major business practice firms will such work support? If you were to ask partners in most of these firms today what percentage of their work is commodity products, I suspect that most would say 10 to 25%. In reality, I think the percentages of commodity products and services for most of the Am Law 200 firms are much higher. However, commodity work with enough at stake cannot be treated by corporate counsel as "commodity work" which may be the salvation of some Am Law 100 firms. While a number of major business practice firms focusing on specialized work will survive, I doubt that there will be enough such work for outside counsel to support 200 or more New York Model firms in the U.S.

There will also be a continuing need for legal services for individuals and small businesses who will find it more cost-effective to employ efficient private-practice legal counsel than to employ a lawyer in-house, full-time, or to undertake laborious regulatory compliance themselves. The legal profession will not disappear, but it will surely continue to change. Some of us will have to find special niches for our services, and many of us will have to accept the fact that the era of pervasive high and easy profits will be a thing of the past.

CHAPTER TWELVE

Technology

Technology has increased competition among legal service providers and facilitated the cost-effective delivery of such services. Continuing improvements in "legal technology" will place downward pressure on the legal costs of clients in the years ahead. What we think of today as "legal technology" has come a long way from 1960 when technology for lawyers consisted primarily of a telephone, an electric typewriter, and the "hot product" of the day—a Thermofax machine that enabled lawyers to make one bad and smelly copy at a time (pink-beige in color and often singed around the edges) of a free-standing page.

Over the past 50 years, we have adjusted first to the Xerox machine in the early 1960s, then to the IBM Selectric magnetic tape typewriter in the late 1960s, then to the primitive fax machine and word processors of the 1970s. The 1980s brought us rapidly improving computerized word processing, much better fax machines, telephones that could patch in multiple parties, and greatly improved and faster document production copiers. During the 1990s most big firms were utilizing available technology to expedite the provision of legal services. The Internet, e-mail, computerized word processing, computerized legal research, cell phones, improved copy and fax machines, pagers, document production systems, and voice mail were among the many examples.

The greatest facilitators and expediters of legal services have been the Internet and e-mail which have virtually eliminated the barriers of distance and time between lawyers, their clients and the other people with whom lawyers deal. Along with laptops, smart phones, and videoconferencing, they have made it possible to send documents in the blink of an eye around the world and to have real time drafting and editing conferences with clients or counsel a continent or an ocean away. This technology makes lawyers more accessible to their clients and reduces the time necessary to respond to clients' needs. It has also greatly reduced the importance of proximity to a working attorney-client relationship. As a result most potential clients in the U.S. are now fair game for any law firm in any city in the U.S., and for other English-speaking lawyers wherever they reside (subject to licensing restrictions that seem to be becoming less important).

Communications technology has also had the effect of removing barriers that formerly protected lawyers from demands by their clients. Now clients often expect a document to be produced immediately upon request and to be completed promptly by the exchange of emailed revisions until the job is done. Lawyers can no longer drop a draft document in the mail and expect a respite of several days during which they can work on other matters. 24/7 e-mail capability and availability does not permit any escape. The result has been an increase in client expectations and, in the process, a significant increase in the pressures borne by lawyers.

Some lawyers are still struggling to catch up with the technology produced in the 1980s while being overrun by the rapidly improving technology of the 1990s and 2000s. The amount of new technology is daunting, and most lawyers and law firms are struggling to sift through all that is available to figure out what to purchase, how to train their personnel, and how to use new technology effectively to produce better and more cost-effective services for their clients.

Clients on the other hand are interested in how technology can reduce the costs of legal services as well as improve them. They have no enthusiasm for paying for their outside firms to acquire and use the latest technology and view its acquisition as a fundamental obligation of the outside firms in the same way that firms were expected to own their own libraries of reference materials in the old days.

It is clear that on one hand the new practice tools and products can be very useful to lawyers and law firms in managing their practices and their "business" operations. On the other hand, it is equally clear that none of these tools can substitute for the value-added role of lawyers as thinkers, explainers, advocates, apologists, and strategists—all of which require thought and reflection. Even though electronics function instantaneously, the human expert still requires time to think and develop a useful response. Nonetheless, it would be unwise for any lawyer, law firm, or corporate law department to ignore these important tools. Without the structure and support provided by these management and production tools, it would be difficult for any lawyer or law firm to remain competitive with the lawyers who are using them wisely.

Some document assembly software products permit lawyers to convert their own forms into semi-automated assembly documents requiring only the answers to a set of questions in order to produce large and complex documents. Nonetheless, the focus and self-discipline required to use these tools effectively is substantial, and many lawyers have not been up to the task, or have made the decision to forego the effort necessary to master these tools in order to maintain their billable hours.

Many firms have pursued knowledge management programs in the expectation of using the program to increase their profitability. Some have not understood that such capabilities are necessary for law firms to survive in the current competitive environment whether they contribute to profitability or not. I think any major firm that wants to stay in business will need an effective knowledge management system. Building and administering a proprietary knowledge management program is expensive and they are not easy to conceive and administer. With the growing availability of good commercial programs most firms will rely on them in whole or in part. If firms don't make the investment in time and money to create or acquire access to such systems, they will be at a considerable disadvantage in seeking to deliver cost-effective legal services that clients will expect.

While I would agree that many of the best lawyers could produce superior documents under optimal conditions, such conditions rarely exist these days. Clients appear to be willing to settle for documents that work and can be delivered promptly, as opposed to more nuanced documents prepared at greater cost over a longer period of time. In order to operate cost-effectively in this environment, I think the gravity of the commercial knowledge management systems will pull us all in.

The experts who talk about the marvels of document assembly software note the incongruence that would result from lawyers investing their time in the adaptation of these tools to their practices, because the tools would then reduce the amount of traditionally billable time that could be charged to the client for the end products. As a result, lawyers might lose the value of the time used to adapt the tool in the first place, and without the client's consent could not charge anything for the time saved in using the software to produce the actual document. However, there is no turning back the clock.

Firms that do not make the investment in technology and the training necessary to use it may find themselves priced out of the market by competing firms that can more cost-effectively produce legal services. Lawyers may ask, "Why should we make such an investment at considerable cost of money and time that will reduce our ability to charge our time to clients?" Again, the answer is *survival.* Your competitors are making these investments; if you don't do it, you will be too slow and too expensive.

The cure advocated by some experts to this economic double-whammy is "value billing," which in this context means charging a fixed fee for a document created by use of a document assembly software system or for research conducted on behalf of another client regardless of the time required to produce it, and this charge would be greater than the value of the time associated with the production of the specific product for a specific client. While this seems logical if the client consents, the profession is faced with the problem of ethical standards adopted in the different technological environment that gave rise to *ABA Formal Opinion 93-379.* This very important Opinion states in part:

> A lawyer who is able to reuse old work product has not earned the hours previously billed and compensated when the work product was first generated; rather than looking to profit from the . . . luck of being asked the identical question twice, the lawyer who has agreed to bill solely on the basis of time spent is obliged to pass the benefits of these economies on to the client. The practice of billing several clients for the same time or work product, since it results in the

earning of an unreasonable fee, therefore is contrary to the mandate of the Model Rules. When that basis for billing the client has been agreed to, the economies associated with the result must inure to the benefit of the client, not give rise to the opportunity to bill a client phantom hours. This is not to say that the lawyer who agreed to hourly compensation is not free, with full disclosure, to suggest additional compensation because . . . the lawyer was able to reuse prior work product on the client's behalf. The point here is that fee enhancement cannot be accomplished simply by presenting the client with a statement reflecting more billable hours than were actually expended.

While the Opinion expressly states that it addresses only issues raised when a lawyer has agreed with a client that the client will be charged on the basis of time expended, the language to the effect that "billing several clients for the same . . . work product . . . results in the earning of an unreasonable fee" should give us some pause. At least, full disclosure of the practice to each affected client would be required, and for those firms that generally bill on an hourly basis, the explanation needs to be complete, and the special arrangement must be specifically agreed to by their clients.

Many clients select the firms they use to take advantage of the firms' accumulated knowledge and document resources, and they usually pay a healthy price for the opportunity to draw on these assets. They generally do not expect to pay a premium over the hourly rate for access to these resources.

In addition, there are client expectations and relations problems with such a "value billing" approach. Clients' interest in reducing their legal costs is as great as lawyers' desire to profit from their work and relationships. Paying lawyers for using cost-savings technology is unlikely to be received well by clients anxious to reduce their legal expenses. I am sure that most clients would understand that a firm is entitled to recover the cost of the product and the training expenses required to use it, spread over a reasonable period of time, but I doubt that any client today would agree that it would be appropriate for each client-user to pay the full price.

Assume for a moment that it was not possible, either ethically or as a practical client relations matter, to sell the same product to different clients at a price in excess of the time necessary to adapt it to each client's use. Would it still be worthwhile for the law firm to develop standardized forms, to acquire access to electronic knowledge management systems and legal research capabilities, and to invest the time necessary to make these programs work? Absolutely! In fact, it will be a necessity to do so regardless of the level of profitability involved, because major clients expect efficiency from their legal service providers.

A law firm can continue to produce just as many billable hours working efficiently as working inefficiently if it has enough clients and work to keep its attorneys fully occupied while working efficiently. While the value of the time should be increased by the effort, lawyers should expect that their clients will want to share in the benefits of increased productivity rather than having all of the benefit accrue to the private practice firms. And the firms that don't become more efficient may lose the work to another law firm that has made the investment or to a New Model firm with lower overhead and rates.

It is very difficult for lawyers and their firms to interrupt the process of creating billable hours to think about learning how to do their work differently and more cost-effectively. At best there is a diminution in the flow of billable work and consequently in income. Will lawyers highly motivated by money have the wisdom and self-discipline to sacrifice in the short term in order to remain competitive in the long term?

As law firms learn how to produce more and better work product in less time, their productivity will increase, and costs to clients of particular products and services should decline. That is what productivity enhancement is all about. And the ability to produce cost-effective legal documents and services should attract clients to the firms and lawyers that can produce them. In the business world customers and clients expect their product and service providers to become more efficient and to reduce the cost of what they sell as they get better at producing it. All of us expect the prices of new technology products (like cell phones, TVs, computers, printers) to go down as production ramps up. Lawyers should not be surprised that clients expect the same of them.

Significantly increased efficiency and productivity in the creation of legal documents and services may over time reduce the need for lawyers just as similar improvements have reduced the demand for travel agents, stockbrokers, journalists, assembly line workers, and architectural draftsmen among others. The increasingly dense and complicated statutory and regulatory environment will generate new legal work to replace some of that eliminated by commoditization and increased productivity. While the law retains a significant amount of intellectual content, some of what we do will be done better by computers and software going forward.

Will IBM's Watson computer displace many young associates (and some older lawyers) in conducting legal research or document review? IBM's general counsel thinks so. " 'Imagine a new kind of legal research system that can gather much of the information you need to do your job—a digital associate, if you will' " he writes in an article for *The National Law Journal*. " 'Pose a question and, in milliseconds, [the program] can analyze hundreds of millions of pages of content and mine them for facts and conclusions.'"[106] Computers have already simplified legal research and document review. In mere seconds, one can search the entire text of lengthy memoranda, contracts, and opinions (or even databases of many legal documents) for particular words or phrases simply by clicking on "Find."

There is no reason to think that further progress will not occur. While significant improvements will not occur overnight, based on the pace of past progress I think we can reasonably expect that substantial additional progress will be made over the next five to ten years. Most of the surviving lawyers will have to learn how to use the best of these new tools to provide legal services more efficiently and cost-effectively. Most of those who do not learn how to use technology to provide more of their services will have to find something else to do.

Once upon a time when Profits Per Partner were much lower, I thought it might be possible with a little luck and a considerable effort for truly productive lawyers to lower their clients' costs and increase their compensation at the same time. I believe that the remarkable increases in PPP over the past 15 years now make that goal impossible. Most lawyers would be very lucky to hold their own.

---

106 *See* John Markoff, *Armies of Expensive Lawyers, Replaced by Cheaper Software*, N.Y. TIMES, Mar. 4, 2011, http://www.nytimes.com/2011/03/05/science/05legal.html?pagewanted=all; Debra Cassens Weiss, *Watson Computer, Making 'Jeopardy' Debut, Could Do Associate Research, IBM GC Says*, ABA JOURNAL (Feb. 15, 2011), http://www.abajournal.com/news/article/watson_computer_making_jeopardy_debut_could_do_associate_research_ibm_gc_sa.

PART III

LOOKING TOWARDS THE FUTURE PRACTICE OF LAW

CHAPTER THIRTEEN

Lawyers Sick of the Practice of Law

The practice of law isn't what it used to be. The transformation of the legal profession in the U.S. chronicled in *Profit and the Practice of Law* and in *Declining Prospects* has not resulted in a happy outcome for many lawyers. The profession that had been substantially transformed into a business by the early 1990s changed even more in the following twenty years and is now very different from what it had been following World War II. How wide spread is the dissatisfaction of lawyers with the practice of law?

The *Raise the Bar* colloquium of the Litigation Section of the American Bar Association was first introduced in this book at the beginning of Chapter Three: Why Working Conditions Have Declined. The principal focus of the colloquium was on lawyers' dissatisfaction with the practice of law. Prior to the first meeting of the colloquium in Chicago in May of 2005, the participants were told that "Young lawyers are unhappy. They work too hard, feel underappreciated, lack mentoring, rarely get trial performance, feel their work is not meaningful, chafe at billable hour goals, have no time for family, flock to irreverent websites that speak too painful truths, don't understand how to or care whether they become partners, and remain on the lookout for their next job." [107]

Participants were also told that senior lawyers were also unhappy. They think that "Young lawyers are overpaid, disloyal, and unappreciative. Competition among law firms has placed Profits Per Partner on an altar that marginalizes all other endeavors – pro bono, bar association activities, training and mentoring." These sentiments are widely shared and often expressed in bar association and other legal profession publications.

The purpose of the colloquium was to find solutions to these problems that could be implemented by law firms. The discussions were sincere, serious and intense. There was no disagreement that serious problems exist within the profession that need to be addressed.

It quickly became apparent that the overriding issue was the relationship between the complaints that were the subject of the meeting and the objective of achieving high Profits Per Partner. It was noted that most of the Am Law 200 firms were committed to the New York Model which has received a lot of attention in this book.

The recurring and pervasive question was the extent to which the Am Law 200 firms would have to forgo or would be willing to forgo some of their Profits Per Partner in order to: provide better training and mentoring, reduce billable hours requirements, enable lawyers to turn off their electronic leashes for a few hours a day and on weekends, provide opportunities to work part-time, and implement other changes that might improve the "quality of life" of their lawyers.

---

107 Brad D. Brian, *Letter to participants in the ABA Section of Litigation's Raising the Bar Colloquium,* March 20, 2005. Some irreverent websites can be found in *Our 100 Favorite Blawgs-For Fun,* ABA JOURNAL (Dec. 2010), at.39.

Among the issues raised were:

1) Can high profits and other values be compatible, and how much profitability is enough?

2) Can an alternative to the New York Model be developed that would maintain an acceptable level of compensation for partners while also alleviating the problems on the table?

3) What business model with clear measures of success can achieve satisfactory work-life balance?

4) What are the responsibilities of the law firm and of the individual lawyers in achieving such a balance?

5) Do law firms recognize that they have problems such as lack of appropriate training, lack of trust among their lawyers, and lack of diversity? If so, do they understand how this impacts their business?

6) What sorts of incentives could be used to solve the problems and how does a firm justify the costs of solving the problems?

7) What are the hallmarks of an effective mentoring and instruction program; how do you define and measure effectiveness; and how do you foster an environment that is effective?

8) How can lawyers prevent their ability to work at any time in any location from becoming a need to work all the time everywhere and to respond instantaneously?

9) How can the administration of justice keep up with technology and avoid being swamped by information?

10) How can lawyers retain the parts of the practice of law that we love in the face of technology and information overload?

After the questions had been identified and stated, it was noted that none of the questions addressed directly the needs and concerns of our clients, who would have to be essential participants in the process. Also missing from the list was the question of the responsibility of the private bar for training and mentoring the next generation of lawyers. It did not come as a surprise that answers to the questions raised were considerably more difficult to find than raising the questions themselves.

The colloquium was divided into smaller groups to discuss the various issues that had been raised. The *Law as a Business Group* felt that it would be necessary to develop new law firm business models as firms sought to bring better balance to the lives of their lawyers. Such new models would have to be realistic in light of the demands of the legal marketplace. The Group recommended that the *Raise the Bar* project seek to identify policies that had worked for firms and those that had failed, in order to develop modes of assistance to law firms and lawyers.

The *Delicate Balance Group* felt that to improve work-life balance for lawyers it would be necessary to make a business case for such balance. It raised the question of whether corporate clients would support the desire for greater work-life balance in private firms just as they were supporting the need for greater diversity. The Group noted that we are all different, and that our ideas of a proper work-life balance vary. In any event, individual lawyers had an important role and responsibility in shaping and controlling their own lives. Finally, the Group felt that firms needed to be honest with prospective associates about the firms' expectations of them in order to better match the needs of the firms and the lifestyles desired by their associates.

There was some debate concerning the role of compensation in the selection of law firms by law school graduates. Most of the lawyers present felt that experience demonstrated that compensation was the dominant consideration. Most law school graduates realized that they would have to work very long hours and would have poor odds of becoming a partner regardless of the firm that employed them. Consequently, many selected their employer from among those that had offered them the highest compensation.

The *Partner and Associates Group* suggested that ten firms be recruited by the project to serve as guinea pigs for an experiment in implementing a *People, Performance and Profit* program similar to the program used by PriceWaterhouseCoopers. It was further suggested that out of these experiments the project would identify "Best Practices" that could then be made available to ABA member firms. The Group also felt that compensation practices for both partners and associates needed to be changed to include in the determination process a variety of things in addition to billable hours, including commitment to diversity, pro bono, practice development, and mentoring and training.

In addition, it was suggested that firms develop a better process for addressing associate concerns, and that associates serve on a joint committee with partners to address these concerns. Such a better process might include "360 Degree" reviews, which would give the associates the opportunity to anonymously evaluate partners.

The *Sink or Swim Group* came up with several suggestions. One was to develop a model mentoring program, and to provide evidence that effective training and mentoring would lead to greater client satisfaction. It also recommended that as a part of each lawyer's annual plan there should be hours set aside for training that each lawyer would be expected to complete, and that would be a part of the total hours expected (including associate attendance on a non-billable basis at "spectator events" such as trials in which they were not participating).

The *Technology Group* recommended that bar associations adopt mandatory CLE requirements that would include a course in managing work, life balance, and technology. Excess work should be recognized as an addiction and treated like alcoholism. Additionally it recommended that law schools have a mandatory course in their curriculum for work-life balance and the use of technology. It was further recommended that law schools give preference to applicants with some prior work experience who had demonstrated management capabilities.

The *Technology Group* also felt that law firms should encourage the use of technology and give credit to efficient lawyers who provided more cost-effective service to clients. The Group further felt that the rules of discovery and the rules governing the use of technology in the courtroom need to be analyzed and refined in light of new technologies. Judges need guidance about the appropriate use of technology in their courtrooms and should not be faced with making ad hoc decisions about what to permit and what not to permit.

When the entire group of participants reconvened a number of additional suggestions were made. One participant, who was a judge, suggested that Am Law 200 firms would do well to examine some of the practices of the plaintiffs' bar. He felt that plaintiffs' firms were much more focused on getting a good result with a small commitment of time than corporate firms. Another suggestion was the creation of an annual award for the firm partner selected by the associates as the best mentor during the year.

In contrast to the interest recently displayed by corporate counsel in the diversity of law firms providing services to their companies, the corporate counsel present were reluctant to involve themselves in the working conditions of associates and partners in the firms they worked with.

One corporate counsel noted that increasingly the services provided by private practice firms were becoming commodities. He was also bold enough to say that corporate counsel were reducing the fees that they would pay to outside firms for commodity work and that outside counsel were going to be chosen by different processes going forward. Indeed, the possibility existed that the process of selecting some legal service providers would soon be moved from the law departments to the procurement departments of some national corporations.

Law firm consultants in attendance provided some minor suggestions for variations on existing practices that could improve the relationships between partners and associates, including better mentoring, the "360" evaluation of partners as well as associates, and more flexible working hours.

In the end, it was acknowledged that the solutions to the problems the colloquium had identified and addressed were beyond the reach of a single meeting. The few pessimists present (including myself) felt it was very unlikely that any "best practices" or "statements of principle" would make any difference in the way Am Law 200 firms ran their organizations. It is my conviction that the problems that gave rise to the colloquium in the first place will be solved only if their solution becomes essential to the survival and profitability of the law firms themselves.

During the course of the following year several other *Raise the Bar* colloquia were held around the country, and in August of 2007 the resulting book *Raise the Bar – Real World Solutions for a Troubled Profession* was published by the ABA Publishing House including my chapter: *Pig in a Poke? The Uncertain Advantages of Very large and Highly Leveraged Law Firms in America*. The book is a thoughtful work worthy of reading by anyone interested in the topic. After a year of additional focus group meetings and face-to-face meeting of lawyers and other professionals of every age, gender, and race, the leaders reported that "We found the sources and nature of unhappiness among lawyers to be almost universal."[108]

---

108 Brad D. Brian, *Foreword*, RAISE THE BAR: REAL WORLD SOLUTIONS FOR A TROUBLED PROFESSION, at vii-viii (ABA 2007).

CHAPTER FOURTEEN

Turning the Clock Back?

I s it possible or desirable to turn the legal profession's clock back to 1960? For many solo practitioners or small firm lawyers things have not changed significantly and almost half of all lawyers in private practice in the U.S. are in solo practice. Many others are in firms with fewer than twenty lawyers. But for the lawyers in larger firms, and especially those in the much larger major business practice firms, many of the advantages of practicing law in the 1960s are irretrievable.

Although in 2011 the major business practice firms were on the whole much larger and their equity partners much better compensated than they had been in the 1990s, the preservation of that prosperity is being challenged by the unfolding conditions of the U.S. economy and in the legal profession. The factors I have addressed in preceding chapters have been changing the fundamentals of legal services and undermining the financial prospects of the major business practice firms. Unsettled financial conditions since 2008 have strengthened the effect of these factors.

Relying on Bureau of Labor Statics numbers, the *ABA Journal* reported in June of 2011 that 22,000 jobs had been lost to the legal sector of the economy since May of 2009 including about 10,000 lawyer jobs.[109] The large U.S. law firms shrank by about 6,600 lawyers in 2009, and lost about 2,900 more lawyers in 2010 on top of a loss of close to 500 lawyers in 2008.[110] It is widely suspected that the layoffs were underreported.[111] White & Case laid off 209 lawyers and 200 staff members, and Latham & Watkins terminated 190 lawyers and 250 staff members in 2009—the largest layoffs reported that year. Orrick is said to have laid off 140 non-partner lawyers or about 20% of its total. Several major firms including Latham were said to have let go 11% or more of their non-partner lawyers.[112] Forty-six percent of the firms responding to *The American Lawyer's* 2010 survey of Am Law 200 firms reported that they had deferred first year starting dates in 2010, but only 17% anticipated doing so in 2011.[113]

---

109 Martha Neil, *Law Jobs Still Lacking: Legal Sector Lost 22,200 in a Year, But Added 300 Last Month*, ABA JOURNAL (June 4, 2010), http://www.abajournal. com/news/article/legal_jobs_still_in_short_supply_despite_signs_of_economic_ recovery/.

110 Debra Cassens Weiss, *BigLaw Lost Nearly 10K Lawyers in Last Three Years*, ABA JOURNAL (Apr. 25, 2011), http://www.abajournal.com/news/article/biglaw_ lost_nearly_10k_lawyers_in_last_three_years.

111　　*See* David Lat, *The State of Biglaw: With Layoffs Down Dramatically, Will Spring Bring Bonuses?*, ABOVE THE LAW (Jan. 25, 2011), http://abovethelaw. com/2011/01/the-state-of-biglaw-layoffs-down-dramatically-so-will-spring-bring-bonuses/; *see also NLJ Numbers Indicate Abundant Stealth Lawoffs*, LAW SHUCKS BLOG (Nov. 10, 2009), http://lawshucks.com/2009/11/nlj-numbers-indicate-abundant-stealth-layoffs/.

112 Debra Cassens Weiss, *Top Layoff List Led by Orrick and Latham*, ABA JOURNAL (Mar. 5, 2009), http://www.abajournal.com/news/article/top_layoff_list_ led_by_orrick_and_latham.

113 Claire Zillman, *The New Normal*, AM. LAW., Dec. 2010, at 66, 66.

DIMINISHING EMPLOYMENT OPPORTUNITIES

The recession came, as all recessions do, at an inconvenient time. It is especially inconvenient for recent law school graduates and law students. The major law firm jobs lost in the Great Recession probably will not return to their former levels when the economy improves. Nonetheless, the number of law schools continues to grow, and the law schools continue to graduate young lawyers in excess of the need for them, while the costs of obtaining law degrees have continued to escalate. Keeping in mind that approximately 44,000 students graduated from law school in 2009, these graduates faced a very difficult job market.

In 2011 the Association of Legal Career Professionals reported that:

> Overall employment nine months after graduation stood at 87.6 percent, the lowest since 1996, when the rate was 87.4 percent. And the report notes that the overall number of "jobs taken"—legal and non-legal—by the class stood at 36,043, nearly identical to the "jobs taken" figure for 2009 (although the number of law graduates increased year to year) .... [O]ne result has been that fewer graduates are entering private practice. For the past 30 years, 55 to 58 percent of new law graduates pursued private practice within nine months of graduation .... This year, only a slight majority—50.9 percent—did so .... The drop in employment would have been even more severe for the class of 2010 if law schools had not created a variety of new employment opportunities for their graduates. Some 2.7 percent of graduates this past

year got a job via a law school program .... Adding
to the dire outlook many more jobs than in previous
years are part-time, temporary, or both—a major
concern for graduates when almost a third of them
are leaving law school with $120,000 in debt ....[114]

The number of law students hired for summer work in 2010
was down about 50%, and only about 70% of this reduced number
of summer associates received offers from the firms for whom they
worked.[115] Many firms have reduced their salaries for their existing
associates as well as for new hires. Starting salaries at many firms
are down from a peak of $160,000 in New York City, and from
about $145,000 to $130,000 in Atlanta and many of the regional
business centers. As a result many law school graduates who are able
to find law firm or in-house jobs were faced with delayed starting
dates and lower compensation than they expected when they made
their financial commitment to a law school education. They are the
lucky ones. Many others are not finding employment as lawyers or
otherwise.

Law school graduates and associates are not the only folks with
troubles in the legal job market. An Altman Weil Flash Survey found
that:

Cuts of equity and non-equity partners will continue in
2011, but at a reduced pace from 2010. Overall, about

114 Julie Triedman, *NALP Report: Law Grad Hiring Reaches Lowest Levels
Since 1996*, AM. LAW. DAILY (June 1, 2011), http://www.law.com/jsp/tal/
PubArticleFriendlyTAL.jsp?id=1202495872960.

115 Debra Cassens Weiss, *As 'Troubling Indicators' Mount for 2010 Law Grads,
an ABA Expert Issues a Warning*, ABA JOURNAL (May 6, 2010), http://www.
abajournal.com/news/article/as_troubling_indicators_mount_for_2010_law_
grads_an_aba_expert_issues_a_war/.

one third of all law firms reported removing non-equity partners in 2010 and more than a third removed equity partners. In 2011, 17% of firms plan to cut equity partners and 21% expect to cut non-equity partners.

Large firms were much more likely than smaller firms to reduce their partnership ranks in 2010 and are more likely to do so again this year. In firms with 250 or more lawyers, 56% cut equity partners and 61% cut non-equity partners in 2010. Twenty-seven percent plan to make cuts in their equity partner ranks in 2011 and 48% will reduce their non-ownership tiers this year.

Firms are taking additional steps to control the number of owners. Twenty-seven percent of firms de-equitized partners in 2010 and 16% will do so again in 2011. Thirty-two percent of firms made fewer partnership offers in 2010 and 18% will do so in 2011. Larger firms are more likely to take these actions than smaller firms.[116]

CHALLENGES FOR MAJOR FIRMS AND FOR CORPORATE COUNSEL

As of early 2011 the recession has clearly and irretrievably put corporate counsel in the driver's seat. As examined in Chapter Seven: Competition, and Chapters Eight and Nine: Costs, there has been a tremendous increase in the available number of capable lawyers as

---

116 Thomas Clay & Eric A. Seeger, *2011 Law Firms in Transition: An Altman Weil Flash Survey,* ALTMAN WEIL, INC., at 2-3.

well as a tremendous run-up in the legal costs of doing business. I do not think that many of the concessions made by law firms in today's environment can or will be recovered when the economy improves. Indeed, I expect that the firms will be required to make many more.

Given the bountiful supply of competent lawyers in the United States, expanded further by access to competent lawyers anywhere through the Internet, and the growing benefits of standardization and commoditization, it is hard to see why corporate law departments would moderate the pressures on outside counsel to further reduce their fees as well as to work more cost-effectively. Currently there are plenty of accomplished lawyers who would be satisfied to live very well (but not opulently). Corporate counsel should be able to maintain the cost reductions already secured and obtain additional concessions.

For corporate law departments there are decisions to be made about issues in addition to the billing rates of outside counsel. They also need to be thinking about how the number of recurring legal issues faced by their companies can be reduced or more cost-effectively addressed. Can better training of company personnel reduce legal claims? Can standardized documents and procedures reduce processing time and mistakes? Can new approaches produce more cost-effective solutions? Can some document preparation and review be outsourced to substantially less expensive service providers in the United States or abroad? Can "alternative" or "New Model" law firms be used to provide very good service at lower costs? Can some of the law department's procurement practices be modeled on the company's other procurement procedures? Can the law department better control the creation, design and marketing of innovative new products and services offered by their companies in order to avoid financial disasters flowing from poorly conceived and managed transactions and products? Collateralized Debt Obligations and

Credit Default Swaps are perfect examples of immature products that were sold into the market before their legal concepts and ramifications had been fully vetted and tested.

What can most major business practice firms expect going forward? The failure of the New York Model to provide cost-effective legal services in most situations and the role of private practice firms have been issues concerning thoughtful lawyers for at least two decades. There have been a number of books written on these issues (*Profit and the Practice of Law* was one of them), and there has been a continuing effort to analyze and address them.

It is likely that there will be a bruising battle among the major business practice firms to remain among the elite expert service providers. Mergers between major firms make sense only if the combining organizations have a strategy that will differentiate their new firm from a significant part of its competition. Just being bigger provides few benefits and many problems. Some big firms that are focused on standardized and commoditized work will likely survive, but it will be very difficult for these firms to maintain their profitability or to combine their commodity practice with an elite expert practice in any of their areas of practice. Some of the commodity practice will migrate to those New Model Firms emphasizing cost-effective and personalized service.

Has the legal profession in the U.S. learned anything from past efforts to refocus and reform the delivery and utilization of legal services? The Law Practice Management Section of the American Bar Association has in the past encouraged efforts to think about the future practice of law. One such effort occurred in November 1999 when the Section co-sponsored with Lotus Development Corporation the *Second Seize the Future* conference. This event focused on the future of the legal profession, with its stated purpose to bring together leaders of the bar to discuss what the future holds for the profession and how to deal with anticipated changes. The conference was billed as "the most powerful and extraordinary gathering for our profession in recent history." While it was a good session and I was glad to participate, it would have been hard for the conference to live up to its advance billing.

On the first day there was an excellent program on innovation presented primarily by Michael W. Harnish of Dickinson Wright PLLC. Mr. Harnish had formerly been Director of Consulting Services for the Midwest United States and Eastern Canada for Lotus Development Corporation. He has also served as chairman of the American Institute of Certified Public Accountants' ("AICPA") Information Technology Executive Committee and as a member of the AICPA's Information Technology Research Subcommittee.

It was clear that Dickinson Wright, with Mr. Harnish's assistance, had applied the available technology to enhance its service delivery capability. Of greater importance the firm had in at least one case succeeded in rethinking, reconfiguring and expanding one of their traditional services to the firm's considerable advantage and to the advantage of its client Chrysler Corporation.

Dickinson Wright had approached Chrysler about expanding the geographic scope of the legal services they rendered to Chrysler in connection with Chrysler's financing of the acquisition of real estate for dealerships. In the process of being told by Chrysler that it was happy with its other counsel, someone picked up on the fact that Chrysler wasn't happy with the overall heavy personnel and financial cost of providing this service to its dealers. The Dickinson Wright team, instead of going back home to practice their presentation skills and to polish the firm resume, started thinking about what they could do to solve Chrysler's problem.

The firm concluded that it should offer to take over the direction and administration of the entire program, not just its legal aspects.

They applied their considerable technological prowess, their intelligence and their organizational skills to solve the entire problem for their client, not just the legal part. The firm made a significant investment of its own time and money in developing a plan that their client might reject out of hand. Most law firms would not take such risk.

Dickinson Wright was able to shorten the average time spent on each acquisition from months to weeks enabling Chrysler to substantially reduce its staff devoted to the activity and Dickinson Wright was rewarded by being allowed to take over this aspect of Chrysler's business nationwide. Another great advantage to the firm was the fact that because of the significant technological and institutional involvement of the firm in the project, no individual partner in the firm could move the work if he or she relocated to another law firm.

The second day of the conclave commenced with a charismatic presentation by Professor Gary Hamel of the Harvard Business School, author of the best-seller *Competing for the Future*. As interesting and challenging as his presentation was, I found it very difficult to convert the ideas he had applied to international industries with a small number of major participants to a profession as extraordinarily fragmented as the legal profession in the United States and the world.

Professor Hamel made clear his view that we live in a world of constant change. He felt that the biggest threat to lawyers is not *inefficiency* but *irrelevancy*. He felt that lawyers were so "caught up in the bonds of legacy" that many of us would not be able to survive, and we could succeed only by changing the rules of the game rather than by executing better what we were doing in 1999. He said it is not enough to *get better*—that we must *get different*.[117]

---

117   Notes of the author taken while attending the Second Seize the Future Conference on Nov. 6, 1999.

In this respect he echoed a basic principal of Professor Michael Porter, the strategy guru who is also a professor at the Harvard Business School (but was not a participant in the conference). One of Professor Porter's basic points is that most of us confuse *strategy* with *operational efficiency*.[118] Most law firms are focused on operational efficiency, which is doing what every other major law firm does, but doing it better. Strategy involves doing something differently from the competition. I think that most law firms have trouble developing a real strategy because it requires a commitment of non-billable time by a firm's partners and a substantial overhaul of their institution—in one word: *RISK*.

Professor Hamel made a chilling reference to the mistake made by the medical profession in surrendering the leadership of the healthcare industry to the insurance companies financing their services rather than controlling the process themselves. Are lawyers also in danger of losing control of their profession?

Perhaps of greatest importance, Prof. Hamel believes that lawyers should be selling solutions to their clients (a la Dickinson Wright–Chrysler) rather than selling law. In his view, the law is just one component of the solutions clients want. We were told that clients don't like the trouble and expense of integrating the legal part of the solution with others to get the result they wanted, and that's probably right for some of them. We were told that our clients would rather buy an entire integrated solution from one source.[119]

The real star of the *Second Seize the Future* conference was Barry Melancon, President of the American Institute of Certified Public

---

118 Michael E. Porter, *What is Strategy?*, Harv. Bus. Rev., Nov.-Dec. 1996, at 61-62.

119 Notes of the author taken while attending the Second Seize the Future conference on Nov. 6, 1999.

Accountants (the "AICPA"). As bold as Daniel in the lion's den he presented the five-year, $20 million program the AICPA called "Vision 2000." The program contemplated that "professional services firms" would provide integrated accounting, actuarial, legal, business consulting and investment banking services.

It was clear that many of the larger organizations that we call accounting firms were thinking of themselves in much more expansive terms, and were planning to provide what Professor Hamel said our clients wanted—a one-stop service capable of providing clients with complete integrated solutions to their problems. At the same time, the legal profession seemed to be saying to its clients: "You can't have what you want. You will have to buy these services piecemeal and integrate them yourselves whether you like it or not!"

James L. Thompson, then President of the Maryland Bar Association, had this impression of the AICPA proposal and the bar response:

> The CPAs have done a very impressive job in recreating themselves and seizing the initiative for the future shape of their profession. We, as lawyers, have done nothing except complain about what the CPAs are doing. We have no vision statement, we have no mission (except to protect the status quo— an impossible task in the information and technology age) and we have taken no bold step to deal creatively with the information and technology revolution. The organized bar must do a better job than this. The penalty for our failure to act will be the same as what happened to the doctors. Another group will seize the future and we will be along for a bumpy ride as

passengers in a vehicle driven by another professional group or business.[120]

We seem to assume that we can prevent our major clients from getting things their own way if we are sufficiently determined and disagreeable about it. While the accountants (should I say "professional services firms") were thinking about how they could add lawyers, business consultants, investment bankers and actuaries to their cast of characters, we have been focusing on how we can prevent them from adding lawyers, and giving little thought to how we could provide the integrated services we are told our clients desire. To do so we would also have to deal with a variety of issues including professional codes of conduct relating to the sharing of fees deriving from such integrated services and the multi-jurisdictional practice of law.

In 1999 the perceived danger to the legal profession was from what we continue to call "accounting firms" which then had started calling themselves "professional services firms." This danger subsided with Enron and the SEC's decision to force the accounting firms out of the consulting business which pretty well put a stop to their ability to provide legal services to their clients in the United States.

I think it is still clear that lawyers and law firm managers need to think seriously about the best way to respond to the preferences of our largest clients. If the AICPA and Gary Hamel are correct in assuming that some clients in some situations will want to purchase an integrated solution to problems (a la Chrysler-Dickenson Wright), the legal profession should take note. It may be too late.

Major business clients now have the power to find their own integrated solutions in a process that would involve the active participation of their corporate law departments rather than one or

---

120 James L. Thompson, *How to Seize the Future, Part 7 (Final) of a Series*, THE COUNTY LINE, Jan. 2002, at 10.

the other of their outside firms. The dominate role of the corporate law department has cut off many private practice law firms from the senior corporate management of their clients and comprehensive involvement in their clients' business affairs. Perhaps it is now the corporate law departments that should be expanding their capability to participate in developing comprehensive solutions to their company's business problems in cooperation with other corporate departments rather than being largely compartmentalized and reactive.

Some law firms have experimented with expanding the range of services they provide to include consulting and lobbying. Others have developed profitable training programs for corporate executives and supervisors that have had the effect of reducing legal claims against their firm's clients (and others). However, the standard major business practice firm has been so profitable in recent years that there has been little incentive to think about doing anything differently. It is difficult to assess whether the U.S. legal profession has any real interest in what the future will bring. Is it too busy realizing on the profit opportunities available today to invest any significant portion of those profits in tomorrow?

Among the deficiencies of the *Second Seize the Future* conference was the absence of most of the major business practice firms, not only from participation in the program, but from attendance at the conference itself. None participated in the presentation of the program and only 6 of the 100 largest firms in terms of gross revenues at the time had a representative at the conclave. Most of the firms that traditionally lead the profession in profitability were nowhere to be seen. Of the top 10 firms in Profits Per Partner, only Robbins Kaplan and Milbank Tweed were represented. The next highest attendee on the PPP list was ranked number 28. I suspect the other top earning firms were busily "Seizing the Future" on their own terms somewhere else and were not interested in sharing their insights on how to do so with the rest of us, or at least did not see the Phoenix conference as the place to do it. Only a handful of corporate counsel were present and only two were on the program. Apparently seizing the future didn't involve corporate counsel either.

There was a lot of talk at *Seize the Future* about being better. We got a number of suggestions about how we could be better marketers, or make better use of technology in order to successfully take legal business away from our competitors, but we got no real insights into what law firms would look like and do in the 21st century that would be different from what we did in 1999. *Seize the Future* did not offer the legal profession a competing vision of its future.

Thirteen years after the 1999 conference, it appears to me that the U.S. legal profession has not been giving much thought to its future. While the American Bar Association addresses many important issues, the issues about the future that are discussed in this book do not top the ABA's list. I think we are failing the "imagination test." We are too accustomed to looking back at the past to find the answers to the challenges ahead of us. The fragmentation of the organized bar into 50 separate state bar associations contributes to the problem. The private practice bar runs the risk of forfeiting its proper role in shaping the delivery of legal services to other forces.

The American Bar Association needs to decide if it is going to take seriously the challenges to the legal profession or continue tinkering with the status quo. If it is serious about "seizing the future," it will need to invest some of the time, effort and money that the AICPA devoted to rethinking the future functions and roles of its members. If nothing else, *Seize the Future* provided a stark contrast between the organized, focused, well-financed and creative Vision 2000 program of the AICPA and the lack of a comprehensive, focused, forward-looking examination of the future of the legal profession by the profession itself. Vision 2000 was a great plan when it was introduced, but fell apart when circumstances changed in the early 2000s. The accountants would have to tell us if they learned anything useful in the process, but we won't know if we can envision our own future and improve it unless we try.

In addition to the issues highlighted in this book, other issues that need to be addressed include the ownership of equity interests in law firms by non-lawyers and the sale to private investors of economic interests in lawsuits. The sale of ownership interests to non-lawyers is about to become a reality in the United Kingdom. Although it is too early to know what the effect will be, I suspect that at least some of the equity partners in major firms would be very interested in selling their equity interests to private investors. Now most retiring U. S. partners are lucky to get their capital back and a meager funded, or a more generous unfunded, pension.

While we have seen the havoc resulting from infusion of investor capital into the investment banking firms, most of which were private partnerships into the 1990s, we do not know how widespread law firm equity ownership could become or how it would affect the profession, the firms themselves, or our clients. A significant and unavoidable result would be the subordination of the interest of our clients to the interest of the owners of our firms. I believe that the results would be even more unfortunate for the legal profession than the results of public ownership have been for the investment banks. It would not be a good thing for our legal system and I hope that it does not occur.

CHAPTER FIFTEEN

New Model Law Firms

Rather than trying to "seize the future," most of America's major business practice law firms are trying to solidify the present. There are good reasons for the firms to be happy with their basic business model and its results. They are not thinking about being different: they like their financial position. For the most part they are thinking about getting better and even more profitable. Unfortunately for many of them, they are vulnerable to continuing competition with corporate law departments as well as to disruptive innovations in the market for legal services that are likely to undermine their profitability.

Corporate law departments continue to grow and to assume responsibility for services previously provided by outside counsel. An Altman Weil fall 2010 survey of corporate law departments found that:

[Such departments] are increasing their internal budgets, hiring more lawyers and paralegals to staff those departments, and decreasing their use of outside counsel . . . .

Sixty-three percent of Chief Legal Officers (CLOs) . . . indicated that they had increased their internal budgets from 2009 to 2010. Forty-one percent plan to hire new in-house lawyers in the next twelve months and 32% will increase the number of paralegals on staff. In the same time period, 29% plan to decrease their use of outside counsel.

These results highlight a shift of perspective among CLOs. Law departments are still going to rely on outside counsel for many things, but they are increasingly serious about finding more cost-effective ways to serve their clients – and that includes adding more internal resources.[121]

The challenges to the major business practice firms from corporate law departments have been addressed in depth in Chapter Nine. For a variety of reasons the major firms have found it difficult to make the adjustments necessary to maintain their competitive position vis-a-vis law departments. Competition among the major firms for the remaining business has been steadily increasing in recent years and is intense.

---

121 *2010 Chief Legal Officer Survey: An Altman Weil Flash Survey,* ALTMAN WEIL, INC., at i.

Virtually all of the major firms have pursued the same basic strategy since the 1970s. A few firms have tinkered around the edges of their policies, but most of them have been more alike than different. Of course, some have executed their strategy more successfully than others, and some markets have been more profitable than others. Elements of luck cannot be avoided. An unusually good or bad result in an important matter can give a firm a boost or set it back.

Technological improvement in communications and the management of legal documents and services in the 1990s decreased the individual lawyer's need for law firm infrastructure and support. It became possible for sole practitioners or small firms to manage document production, access practice resources, and to communicate with clients without a staff of assistants, a physical library, or an office. As a result individuals or small groups were able to provide some of the legal services required by clients at a reduced cost. Over time these developments and others have enabled the creation of new types of legal service providers and attorney-client relationships, and they have also altered the market structure of the legal services industry. Out of these modest beginnings, "New Model" law firms began to appear and many established smaller firms found themselves better able to compete with their major firm competitors.

The New Model firms are different. Most of them have in common lower leverage, smaller size, lower overhead, and lower billing rates or other fee arrangements. The average experience level and age of their lawyers are often higher than those of the major firms. As a result their clients receive more or most of their legal advice from mature and experienced lawyers. Some of the firms are very small; most are less hierarchical than New York Model firms. The most rudimentary of these firms are sole proprietorships focusing on a limited set of services.

I was very surprised recently when a younger former colleague paid me a visit and told me of his work for three of the most important national businesses headquartered in Atlanta that use his legal services as a sole practitioner with no support staff for a limited range of important but frequently used agreements. By specializing and being very good at producing a few types of recurring documents, he had laid the basis for a comfortable law practice. My surprise did not relate to his talent, which is high, but rather to the fact that a sole practitioner without major firm support or partnership credentials could attract and hold such clients for an important aspect of their business.

Another type of New Model firm is referred to as the "virtual" law firm. Such firms consist of two or more independent lawyers connected by the internet and telephone who collaborate on and refer work to one another. These firms normally do not have firm offices (each participant usually has an office in his or her home). Many of them have no staff and do their own document preparation. The "partners" in these firms range from recent law school graduates who have not found a better position to retired lawyers who want to remain active and earn some income. There are numerous possible combinations in between. Some of these groups have firm offices and some have support staff.

There are also New Model firms that are larger and more sophisticated competitors of the major firms. These firms are becoming a major source of "disruptive innovation" in the legal services industry. Professor Clayton Christensen of the Harvard Business School has written about this concept in *The Innovator's Dilemma*.[122] He explains the paradox of well-managed, market-leading businesses that listen to their customers, understand their competitors and invest heavily in

---

122   Clayton M. Christensen, The Innovator's Dilemma (HarperBusiness 2000).

new technologies nonetheless failing when confronted with disruptive changes in technology and market structure. One such change is "performance oversupply" which occurs when the product or service offered to clients exceeds the clients' requirements. Although *The Innovator's Dilemma* focuses primarily on manufacturing enterprises, I think that much of Professor Christensen's analysis applies to the legal profession as well.

Most of the major business practice firms are focusing their resources on the most profitable legal work and are selling services that exceed the requirements of some of their clients. Many have moved up-market and in the process they are vacating some of the sectors of the legal market that are less profitable to them and giving New Model and smaller firms the opportunity to undertake the work that they have forsaken. As a result some long-standing clients are left behind either deliberately or as a result of higher charges that the clients are unable or unwilling to pay.

Opportunities that are too small to excite the larger firms can be of great interest to smaller firms. The large firms may as a consequence miss emerging opportunities that have significant growth potential. When law firms provide their clients with a level of service they do not need, they will ultimately find that the clients are unwilling to pay for it. In short, "[t]hey give [clients] more than they need or ultimately are willing to pay for."[123]

Performance oversupply is a widespread feature of today's market for legal services and products. This was a principal point of Mark Chandler's comments in his speech to the Northwestern Securities Regulation Institute conference in January of 2007 to the effect that: "winners will be those who are able to standardize services to meet

---

123   *Id.* at xix.

clients' cost management and predictability needs where very good is good enough."[124]

Many of the legal products and services offered by the major business practice firms today are more than "very good" and cost more than "very good" products and services should. These conditions give the New Model firms an opportunity to establish themselves in the market and to expand their range of services while improving their financial performance. The major firms on the other hand find that the remaining market for their services is smaller and they are forced to engage in intense competition with other major firms for the available business. Firms that are able to offer a legal service that is closer to what the client needs can gain a foothold in the market by doing so. In order to gain such a foothold, New Model firms must be innovative, flexible and willing to forego some profit that they might otherwise make.

Professor Christensen is not alone in identifying situations where low-cost providers can upset premium players in the market place. Adrian Ryans has written in the *McKinsey Quarterly* about companies underestimating low-cost rivals. "Executives always regret it when they don't anticipate the scope of a low-cost threat and respond forcefully. To be sure, a failure to see competitors is an example of the forces of 'creative destruction' at work in capitalism."[125] Mr. Ryans further states that:

---

124 Chandler, Gen. Counsel of Cisco Sys., Inc., Address at the Northwestern School of Law Securities Regulation Institute: State of Technology in Law (Jan. 25, 2007), *available at* http://blogs.cisco.com/news/cisco_general_counsel_on_state_of_technology_in_the_law/.

125 Adrian Ryans, *When Companies Underestimate Low-cost Rivals*, McKinsey Quarterly (June 2010), http://mkqpreview1.qdweb.net/article_page.aspx?ar=2578.

Premium companies may very well have low production costs, but their full costs, with all complexity and overheads, are rarely as low as those of a low-cost player, even though they may have greater scale.

. . . .

Competing successfully in the good-enough segments of a market (as well as holding on to premium customers) may require very different business systems, not just different products or services.

. . . . Developing and implementing the new strategies is a huge challenge for any management team. Yet before they can be formulated, the team must work hard to detect changes in customer needs and behavior—which . . . is a task some premium-brand incumbents have failed at time and time again.[126]

Many New Model firms and some established smaller firms will be successful because their major firm competitors are wedded to their high overhead and their desire to be players in the most remunerative and competitive part of the legal services market. By comparison, their New Model competitors seek to be more responsive to the cost and service concerns of corporate counsel by being good partners—reducing costs, seeking efficiencies, working collaboratively, and finding creative ways to meet the legal service requirements of their clients. We know this strategy is working successfully at my own firm, Taylor English Duma LLP, because of the rapid growth of our client base as we provide many services previously supplied to companies

126 *Id.*

by our major business practice competitors. Other examples of New Model firms include Clearspire and FSB FisherBroyles LLP.

In order to take advantage of such opportunities in the market place for legal services, some of the more sophisticated New Model firms (as well as some of the established smaller firms) operate in a more traditional manner with appropriate offices and support staff. They often have a substantial litigation focus, in part because of the importance of the reputation and prior experience of individual lawyers in litigation matters, and in part because their corporate clients are less likely to have the requisite litigation experience.

New Model firms typically lack the resources necessary to manage the largest corporate transactions or the most complex litigation that require dozens of lawyers operating on tight schedules. However, depending on the experience of their particular lawyers and the depth of their practice groups, some New Model firms can handle sizable and complex matters in their areas of expertise, and provide the legal services required by all but the largest transactions.

The strategy pursued by almost all of the major business practice firms over the last three decades has focused more on maximizing the profits of the firms' controlling partners rather than on maximizing the value of service to clients. The strategy of some of the more mature New Model firms is to use the opportunity provided by the current supply/demand environment to provide services that place a greater emphasis on client value. They do so by providing legal services at better prices and more in tune with the needs of modern day law departments and other clients.

New Model firms have been able to attract seasoned lawyers from a wide range of legal service providers. Many are lawyers who believe that they can build a better, more sustainable law firm which in the long term will provide them with a sufficiently profitable and more satisfying practice. Some New Model lawyers have chosen to leave their major firms because they realized that their clients would ultimately leave them—not because of the quality of their service, but because the clients would not be willing or able to continue paying the major firm's ever-increasing rates. New Model firms have provided some of these lawyers the opportunity to retain their clients and often to grow the volume of work available from them.

Like other corporate executives many corporate counsel are required from time to time to relocate their families in order to move to a higher level of responsibility in their organizations, or they may become redundant because of mergers or business failures. New Model firms can provide good lawyers caught up in these circumstances an attractive alternative.

Some lawyers seek a better opportunity than the one provided by their current firms for any one of several good reasons. A lawyer's particular talents or expertise may be mismatched with the practice of his existing firm, or his firm may be overloaded with the expertise he can provide thereby diluting the opportunities for all in his group. He may not have a good relationship with one or more important partners.

New Model firms have also benefited from the recent retirement or displacement of many capable and experienced attorneys by major firms. In order to maintain their PPP most major firms effectively compel their partners to retire or to take nonequity status at the age of 65 or earlier despite the fact that many of them are living longer in good health and are not ready to fully retire.

Firms have also forced out able lawyers before their retirement age when their practices contracted during the Great Recession—even if their practices subsequently recovered. After such a decision has been made it is hard to undo without reconsidering other personnel decisions. Many of these lawyers have been pleased to find that their clients were delighted to continue using their services at their new firm—sometimes at the same hourly rate. As a result there is a rising number of highly competent and experienced lawyers in New Model firms who are able to compete against their former firms and others with lower overhead and lower leverage that permits them to provide their services at a lower cost.

While it is unlikely that a New Model firm would be able to provide its services to a business client at a lower cost than its own law department, they can significantly reduce the gap between the cost of corporate counsel and many outside alternatives; by doing so they improve the odds of being hired.

Taylor English emphasizes experienced and capable lawyers, low leverage, and low overhead. Approximately two-thirds of our lawyers have 15 years or more of practice experience (for some, this includes in-house experience) and most of the senior lawyers have a sufficient client following to keep themselves busy and to generate a more than adequate income. We currently have over 100 lawyers, only a third of whom would be classified as associates in other firms. The rest are partners or counsel. Rather than having a ratio of one partner or counsel for each two, three or four associates, we have approximately two partners or counsel for each associate. The firm is organized with traditional departments and teams of lawyers providing services to clients in a collaborative manner.

Many New Model firms are able to charge their clients one-third to one-half less than their major business practice competitors while producing generous incomes for their lawyers. Comparatively low overhead allows them greater freedom to structure fees because there is no need or requirement to maximize profit on every engagement. As a result, their lawyers are free to place caps on fees, to agree to fixed fee and flat fee arrangements, and to structure "success fees" on a variety of legal matters. They personally reap the benefits or suffer the consequences of their own decisions. Most major business practice firms cannot allow such discretion because of their high overhead and PPP requirements.

The major firms have to date been able to increase their billable rates and maintain the profitability of their practices because many corporate law departments have not yet been convinced that New Model firms and established smaller firms can consistently deliver very good service at a lower price. To become a major force in the U.S. legal services business, the New Model law firms will have to convince law departments that they have the necessary expertise, skill, judgment, depth and reliability to represent their clients well. Some have been successful in doing so. As the New Model firms establish themselves on a sounder footing the dominance of many of the major firms will be further undermined.

In the headlong rush to higher profitability, I think that many of the major firms are failing to invest enough effort in building their organizational capabilities and relationships. Those firms relying heavily on lateral partners may be more inclined to make this mistake. Because so many lateral entry partners have not grown up within their firms, they are inclined to underestimate the value of the firm's intellectual, professional and managerial history and infrastructure; the success of the laterals within their new firms devalues these same assets to the lifers. This is one of the dynamics that is creating opportunities for New Model firms.

Cox Communications has been a happy user of the services of small and medium sized law firms. James A. Hatcher, the recently retired General Counsel of Cox, wrote an interesting article for the March 2010 edition of *ACC Docket* entitled *Managing Outside Counsel: Using Law Firm Networks to Help Find Value with Small and Mid-Sized Firms.*[127] Mr. Hatcher disclosed that Cox had been using small

---

127 James A. Hatcher, *Managing Outside Counsel: Using Law Firm Networks to help Find Value with Small and Mid-Sized Firms*, ACC Docket (Mar. 2010).

and mid-sized firms from across the country for decades and with considerable satisfaction and success. He said: "you can frequently find small to mid-sized firms with the resources and specialized expertise required for large legal matters of critical importance to the company. Consider the qualifications of the firm regardless of size."[128]

In order to find the right firm for a particular job, he recommended his preference for relying on someone else to do the initial screening—an alliance or network of law firms. Among the alliances and networks mentioned were the International Society of Primerus Law Firms and the National Association of Minority & Women Owned Law Firms. "Each of these alliances heavily screens their member law firms for characteristics including quality work product, integrity, commitment and reasonable fees."[129]

On one hand I am not surprised that many corporate law departments have been slow to employ sole practitioners, virtual law firm lawyers, smaller firms and New Model firms to provide services to them. On the other hand I know that there are many very competent lawyers working in smaller firms including New Model firms who are finding better and less expensive ways to serve the needs of their clients. I am pleased to be a partner in one of these firms.

My former partner Bill Jacobs summed up the New Model phenomenon this way:

> The New Model is, I think a healthy alternative that will likely thrive, and while it will pressure the large business firms I don't expect it to replace the traditional model. To some extent there is a symbiotic relationship—New Model firms need lawyers who

---

128 *Id.* at 93.

129 *Id.*

have gained experience in the big firms, and perhaps the potential for that avenue of future employment assists the big firms in attracting the entry-level associates they need for their model. A key for GCs facing novel and important issues is to select counsel with seasoned judgment, creativity, breadth of experience, and analytical capabilities. I think the traditional firms will continue to have a perceived advantage with respect to such qualities and will enjoy a significant success in marketing this advantage that will keep many of them going, even as established (albeit not necessarily commoditized) forms of work may be migrating to the New Model.[130]

I agree with Bill that a number of major business practice firms will survive and prosper for the reasons he noted, but the more sophisticated New Model firms are already competing for some of the most important legal work. The best lawyer or firm for a particular challenging task is not always the most expensive one. While all of us are motivated by the desire to be fairly compensated for our efforts, it is becoming increasingly difficult to find at the same law firm both the highest possible economic return and a stable, satisfying and amiable working environment. Many talented New Model lawyers are choosing the latter over the former.

---

130 E-mail from William S. Jacobs, Gen. Counsel, EMS Technologies, to author (Dec. 31, 2010) (on file with author).

CHAPTER SIXTEEN

The Future of Lawyers?

This book has had a lot to say about conditions in the practice of law, especially in the major business practice firms, in the past and present (economics, style of practice, disappointments and rewards), and I have made some predictions about the future. What questions arise from all this for the individual reader? For younger lawyers some of the vital questions are: What do I want to do with my career and my life? Can I expect to earn a seven-figure income from my practice? How can I manage my legal career for my personal and financial satisfaction? How should I steer my law firm for success? Should I change specialties? Should I change law firms? Should I leave the profession for another career path? For many college students the question is: Should I go to law school? These questions cannot be answered without a hard look at the future.

There are deep ruts in the roads traveled by most lawyers and law firms. All attorneys have been educated to respect and honor precedent and we like to stick to past patterns. But waves of change are washing over the legal profession and they require close attention. The past can no longer teach you all you need to know.

Why do people want to go to law school? There are a wide variety of reasons. Maybe they've admired a family friend who was a well-regarded judge or lawyer, or they've watched a lot of *The Practice* and *Boston Legal* on TV. Or perhaps they believe law will provide a path to serve the public interest or to a seat in their state legislature or the U.S. Congress. Some go to law school because they cannot find a better option after college, particularly in recent times. Some have heard that it is a relatively easy way to earn a lot of money and want to do so.

Many law school aspirants hope to earn a substantial income and enjoy the life money brings. Is this realistic? Yes for some, but too many law school graduates have trouble finding any legal jobs, much less the high paying major firm jobs that are in short supply. Many of those that do find jobs cannot earn enough income to pay back the debts they incurred with their legal education. In 2010 out of the 1,225,000 lawyers admitted to practice in the U.S. only about 83,000 were employed by the Am Law 100 firms (about 7%) of whom about 19,000 (1.5% of the total lawyers in the U.S.) were equity partners.[131] With 44,000 plus students graduating from law school each year, the chances of becoming an equity partner in such a firm are slim indeed and getting slimmer every year.

Many law graduates have trouble passing the bar; some never do, but they nevertheless owe their law school loans. Those who have done very well in law school will usually find jobs, but to really get ahead in the future as a lawyer they are going to need talents that go beyond what good lawyers have been taught in law school and have needed in the past.

---

131 Robin Sparkman, *Back in Black*, Am. Law., May 2011, at 79, 79.

There will be a continuing need for a lot of lawyers to serve the individual, family and small business markets. These clients have largely been dropped by the major business practice firms. Some major firms have abandoned their estate practices entirely. The lawyers and small law firms serving these markets will continue as before, much like individual accountants and small accounting firms service similar markets.

However, even this end of the market for legal services will be affected by improved access to information and resources about legal issues. Some individuals and small businesses will be able to familiarize themselves with basic legal issues and procedures and to deal with them satisfactorily without professional assistance. For example software programs and online services are available that enable individuals and small businesses to prepare and file their own tax returns with a reasonable prospect of correctness, or to write their own wills (admittedly they aren't perfect, but some lawyers' wills aren't either). Individuals can now form their own corporations on government websites without professional assistance, and basic forms and instructions on this subject and many others are readily available in book stores or on the internet. Much of this knowledge is accessible and useable by anyone with a college or a good high school education.

This book has mainly been concerned with the major business practice law firms and their lawyers: how they got to where they are in the present, and where they are likely to be in the foreseeable future. I have tried to address the primary issues that will be faced by these firms and their lawyers in the near term. I believe that there will be a substantial reduction in the ability of many major firms to generate extraordinary Profits Per Partner. The de-financialization of the U.S. economy and the deflation of the real estate bubble are significant adverse economic factors affecting the firms. It is uncertain if the economy will recover its appetite for the complex specialized legal work that has been the bread and butter of so many of the major business practice firms for the last decade or more. There will be an accompanying impact on the incomes to which the partners in many such firms have become accustomed.

The extraordinary profitability of the big law firms has continued to attract to the legal profession thousands upon thousands of smart, industrious, and ambitious lawyers. At the same time, in-house general counsel are realizing that there is an over-abundant supply of capable lawyers available to do most of the work they require, and that the costs of the services they purchase should be declining rather than increasing. More and more of the work being done by the major firms is being commoditized, and in the process the intrinsic value of many of their services has declined.

College graduates assessing their future need to think seriously before pursuing a legal career. They need to think about what they want for themselves and their families. They need to consider the cost in money and years of their lives of pursuing a law degree. There are going to be fewer jobs at the big business practice law firms, and a small percentage of the 44,000 plus graduates from law school each year will be able to land jobs with such firms. Some of the jobs they do land may not offer partner track opportunities.

Law graduates who are graced with an offer from a major firm need to decide if they want to make the lifestyle sacrifices necessary to be successful in such a job. Competition for the higher level legal positions in such firms will be ferocious and is likely to encourage the equity partners of the major firms to take advantage of the swarms of able and ambitious young lawyers trying to enter the coveted ranks of equity partners.

As the major firms reduce their leverage, a higher percentage of their smaller associate classes may find a life-long career with their firms. As a result there will be fewer trained private practice associates available to staff in-house legal departments. Some corporate law departments are beginning to realize the necessity and desirability of training their new lawyers themselves. Frankly some of the habits and skills learned in private practice are more of a liability in-house than an asset. Law schools should consider adding a few courses to help students prepare for direct entry into corporate law departments.

The huge increase in legal service costs is requiring that chief executive officers find corporate general counsel who can manage and control such costs, and increasingly the general counsel will do so. If general counsel cannot manage their law departments as business executives, they may find themselves reporting to a non-lawyer executive at the head of their law department.

The future and fortunes of most of the major business practice firms and their lawyers are now in the hands of corporate counsel. Major businesses will find a way to reduce the cost of their required legal services. Some New Model law firms are developing better *service/cost/quality* equations for much of the legal work required by business. These New Model firms will be able provide many of the legal services that most businesses require from outside counsel at a noticeably lower cost. As a result, I believe the New York Model for most major firms will not continue to produce the extraordinary financial results of recent years. A few of the firms with the most expertise and sound strategies may be able to maintain their recent very high levels of compensation, but overall large firm profitability is destined to decline in the face of increasing competition (from private practice law firms and corporate law departments), disaggregation, commoditization, outsourcing, technological advances and other changes in the market for legal services.

One of the advantages of our capitalistic system is that it can adjust rapidly to economic imbalances and develop alternative and more frugal ways to provide services. The high end of the U.S. legal profession is very likely to be its latest victim. The conclusions reached by my analysis are not based on any resentment of the profitability of practicing attorneys in the major firms in recent decades; I have been a beneficiary of some of that profitability myself. Nor do I ignore the historic traditions of the legal profession and its place in the American experience. Highly profitable financial activities attract large numbers of potential participants which inevitably dilutes the value of the opportunity. Few if any exceptionally good things last forever.

My conclusions are based on the laws of supply and demand, the flexibility of free markets, and the intellect and experience of corporate counsel whose companies are the primary consumers of premium legal services. The forces of competition, rising costs and commoditization, coupled with strong corporate law departments and advancements in technology and communications inevitably lead to declining prospects for the major business practice firms and their lawyers.

EPILOGUE

As I was completing the manuscript of *Declining Prospects*, the news of partner defections and financial woes emanating from Dewey & LeBoeuf became dire, and on May 28th, 2012, this internationally prominent law firm that once employed 1,400 lawyers filed for bankruptcy.

In the last two decades we have seen the collapse of a number of our largest and best known law firms including Brobeck, Coudert Brothers, Arter & Hadden, Heller Ehrman, Thacher Proffitt, WolfBlock and Howrey. Other major firms facing financial difficulties have merged to avoid the risk of collapse.

The prominence of Dewey has led to unusual front-page media interest in the economics of large law firms and the question: "How could such important institutions fail?" Although I did not have Dewey in mind over the past two years while writing *Declining Prospects*, I am confident that my analysis of the economics and culture of today's major law firms answers the question. Dewey like most of the other failed firms was caught short by fundamental changes in the dynamics and economics of the top end of the legal profession that are the focus of *Declining Prospects*.

Why have some of our most revered law firms fallen to pieces? Important contributing factors are 1) greatly increased competition, 2) client resistance to increasing costs, 3) the growth in size and importance of corporate law departments, 4) commoditization of legal services, and 5) technological change. Of all these factors the most important reason for the failure of Dewey & LeBoeuf is intense competition among private practice law firms to provide the legal services required by major businesses.

In order to find enough high-paying business to meet the compensation expectations of its partners, Dewey aggressively recruited high-billing partners from other prominent firms by guaranteeing them high incomes. This is a risky strategy because Rule 5.6 of the American Bar Association's Model Rules of Professional Conduct (adopted by most state bars) contributes significantly to the instability of major law firms: the effect of the rule is unlimited free agency for lawyers. Thus high-billing partners (who have already shown a willingness to abandon their colleagues for more money elsewhere) always remain free agents able to leave with their clients in response to the lure of a better offer. Granting guaranteed income to newcomers naturally offends existing partners who do not have such guarantees and often (as in the case of Dewey) causes them to demand such guarantees for themselves. And sometimes some of the anticipated new business fails to materialize or goes unpaid.

Two other changes affecting law firm dynamics and economics have loosened partner bonds to their law firms and further facilitated free-agency. The first is the widespread availability of malpractice insurance which makes it less important to know and to have confidence in the ability, judgment and integrity of your partners.

The second is the legalization of limited liability partnerships which protect partners from firm liabilities other than their own malpractice. With no fear of personal liability for their law firms' liabilities, the individual partners have far less reason to oppose the borrowings that can result from expansion and partner income guarantees. Although the partners in small and medium-sized firms usually have to guarantee their firms' loans and leases, apparently lenders and landlords have been willing to lend and rent to large firms without such guarantees.

In Dewey's case, public attention has been focused on enumerating mistakes that the firm made that led to its demise: Dewey had too much debt; Dewey hired too many lateral partners; Dewey had guaranteed too many of them too much compensation; Dewey paid its most highly compensated partners far more than many of its other partners. But most of the commentary missed the ultimate question: "What caused Dewey to make these mistakes?" The answer, I think, boils down to the stresses of competition for business. Dewey could not generate enough legal business at high enough prices to meet the income expectations of its partners. Most of the actions identified as "Dewey's mistakes" were a result of its desperate efforts to meet these expectations. It was unable to do so.

Increased competition among law firms is a result of a significant increase in the number of capable lawyers and law firms competing for the available legal business. The law schools have contributed to this excess supply by graduating many more able and ambitious young lawyers than there are opportunities for them in the practice of law.

At the same time business clients are seeking to reduce their cost of legal services by bringing legal work in-house and are becoming less dependent on private practice law firms. They have discovered that major firms are willing to compete for business by lowering the prices of their services. These conflicting priorities of private practice firms seeking to increase revenue while their clients seek to economize are bound to collide, and clients have the upper hand.

Many of the major firms, including Dewey, also have made significant unfunded promises of retirement income to their partners and retired partners. Many younger partners ask why these pensions were not fully funded at the time the firms were paid for the services rendered. They see these obligations much the same way as the taxpayers of towns and states all over the United States see underfunded pension and health care obligations to the retired employees of their police departments and school systems.

Given the extreme mobility of lawyers in the legal profession, if a firm borrows money to meet its compensation commitments on top of its unfunded pension obligations, it is going to be difficult to keep the young and ambitious partners and lawyer-employees around: many have other options without these burdens. If a firm is unable to pay its star lateral and legacy partners what they have been promised, they are likely to leave. Once a firm starts to unravel there is no turning back.

Because partners must pay income taxes on their earnings whether they take them out each year or leave some in their firms to increase their capital, there are few law firms that have a substantial base of invested capital. Consequently many major firms borrow most of their working capital and distribute to the partners as much of their earnings as possible on a current basis. The temptation to borrow money to make distributions to the partners is always present. Optimism about the collectability of a firm's receivables is often viewed through rose-colored glasses. Such borrowings are almost always a certain path to collapse.

Banks and law firms can protect themselves and discourage such moves by partners from one firm to another by requiring that each partner guarantee all or some portion of the firm's obligations proportional to the partner's economic participation in the firm. Lessors can do the same. If they did so, fewer firms would fall apart. But doing so would require that all of the partners commit themselves to their firms, and many are not willing to do so.

The competitive pressure on the major firms is also being increased by the commoditization of legal services and their outsourcing and off-shoring. Further advances in technology are making it easier for clients to use a wider array of law firms and for more law firms to produce "good enough" legal work. New Model law firms that are happy to compete on price will undercut the high priced services of many major firms.

Can firms do anything to combat these perils? The small number of truly elite firms may have the answer: most have only one class of partner, they have eschewed lateral hiring, they have focused on high quality service rather than on volume, many have remained relatively small, and they have been very cautious in expanding.

Unfortunately it appears inevitable that increased competition and the other changes in the dynamics and economics of today's legal world discussed in *Declining Prospects* will over time cause many other major business practice firms to succumb to Dewey's fate.

THE END

21155248R00149

Made in the USA
Lexington, KY
01 March 2013